Praise for *The Five-Minute Miracle*

"Short. Simple. Specific. The miracle occurs when you take on this practice. Thank you, Tara!"

–Mary Anne Radmacher,
author of *Live Boldly* and *Simply an Inspired Life*

"*The Five-Minute Miracle* has the power not only to transform the quality of your life and bring you much greater peace, love, happiness, and joy, but to heal your relationships, manifest your dreams, clarify your soul's purpose and contribute to the healing of the world. Do yourself and your loved ones a favor and buy it now."

–Philip H. Friedman, PhD, director of the
Foundation for Well-Being and author of
Creating Well-Being and *The Forgiveness Solution*

"Tara Springett's higher consciousness healing technique, shared in *The Five-Minute Miracle*, is a practical and priceless gem. Each of us can benefit from adding this technique to our treasure chest of healing skills."

–Sue Patton Thoele, author of *The Courage to Be Yourself*
and *The Mindful Woman*

THE FIVE-MINUTE MIRACLE

THE FIVE-MINUTE MIRACLE

Discover the personal healing symbols
that will solve your problems

Tara Springett,
founder of Higher Consciousness Healing

WEISERBOOKS
San Francisco, CA / Newburyport, MA

First published in 2010 by
Red Wheel/Weiser, LLC
With offices at:
500 Third Street, Suite 230
San Francisco, CA 94107
www.redwheelweiser.com

ISBN: 978-1-57863-458-3

Library of Congress Cataloging-in-Publication Data is available upon request.

Cover and text design by Kathryn Sky-Peck.
Typeset in Garamond BE.
Printed in the United States of America
TS
10 9 8 7 6 5 4 3 2 1

Text paper contains a minimum of 30% post-consumer-waste material.

CONTENTS

Acknowledgments

I want to thank my agent Lisa Hagan and my publisher Jan Johnson for believing in me and my work. A big thank you goes to the entire team at Red Wheel for making my manuscript into a beautiful book. I feel deepest gratitude to all my Buddhist teachers and, in particular, Rigdzin Shikpo and Garchen Rinpoche. They guided me safely around all the pitfalls that lay on the spiritual path and taught me how to find love—first in myself and then with others. Deepest thanks to Wally Sawford, who is a very special Buddhist and Taoist teacher. He introduced me to meditation experiences that inspired me greatly. Thanks also to all my psychotherapeutic teachers—most of all Phyllis Krystal, from whom I learnt about the amazing effectiveness of symbols in the therapeutic process. Thank you to all my clients who had the trust and the courage to try a new method and who shared their processes with me. And finally, thanks to my husband and soul-mate, Nigel, who readily tried higher-consciousness healing as soon as I discovered it and who supported me in every way. Without his generous help, this book would not have been written.

INTRODUCTION

IN 1997, I HAD AN EXPERIENCE that changed my life forever. I was sitting in the shrine room of my Buddhist teacher trying to listen to his talk. I could not concentrate, because I was inwardly struggling with a painful feeling of sadness that had been with me for many years. As I had often done before, I prayed for help and—lo and behold!—this time, my prayer was answered. Suddenly, the method described in this book just "popped up" in my mind. It was so clear and detailed that I assumed I had read it somewhere and was just remembering it. In the weeks and months that followed, I successfully used this method to dissolve my sadness and many smaller issues as well.

I then introduced the method to my friends and family, and later to my clients. I carefully monitored their individual processes and asked them to measure their success on a scale. The results were overwhelming. I have worked with many hundreds of cases and virtually *every single person* who has used this method has achieved significant improvement with a wide variety of problems within a few days or weeks. What's more, many people have told me that they achieved wonderful results all by themselves, simply by learning the method from this book. Most important, these improvements were stable and lasting. Higher-consciousness healing seems to have the power to resolve personal problems without lengthy analysis and without having to relive past traumas.

When I look back, it seems as if much of my life had been leading up to this experience—it had prepared me to "receive" this method, refine it, and then make it accessible to others. Thirteen years earlier, I had found

Tibetan Buddhism, coming to it like a lost child running into its mother's arms. Since the very first time I visited the Buddhist center, I have meditated every day for at least an hour. I have spent virtually all my vacations in intensive teaching and meditation retreats with knowledgeable and experienced teachers who guided me along the way. Over the years, a deep motivation evolved in me: I wanted to develop enough happiness, insight, and love in myself that I could be of real benefit to other people.

A few years after I started to meditate, I began to work as a counselor and psychotherapist, trying to put my desire to help other people into practice. I had completed several long-term counseling trainings and had earned qualifications, so I felt that my ability to help had grown considerably. However, after working as a psychotherapist for a few years, I began to wish I could find a more effective technique to help my clients than the one I had been using. Ideally, this method would be very simple, so that everyone could use it as a self-help tool. It would bring reliable results every time it was used. In addition, I wanted a method that would point people to the eternal truth that true happiness can be found only through the awakening of a loving heart.

When I discovered higher-consciousness healing, I had no idea that it represented exactly the ideal method I sought. Only when one person after another saw positive results from the method did I slowly become convinced that I had been given a real gem.

The core of higher-consciousness healing is, quite simply, to make contact with our higher consciousness—the part of our mind that is more loving and wise than our everyday consciousness. If we follow a spiritual path, we may choose to perceive our higher consciousness as a central figure of our religion or tradition. However, we do not need to be religious or spiritual in order to benefit from higher-consciousness healing. The essence of our higher consciousness is altruistic love—a form of love that is available to everyone, regardless of whether they are spiritual.

Higher-consciousness healing will help us communicate with our higher consciousness and make its wisdom and love available to solve our personal problems. We will receive this help by using symbols. These symbols, when visualized regularly for just four minutes a day, have an amazing power to transform. They can reach deep into our unconscious mind and put things right at their root. We don't even need to know all the intricate causes of our problem, because higher-consciousness healing focuses entirely on the solution. The practice is absolutely safe, and we can achieve a significant decrease in our suffering from almost every type of problem in a matter of days or weeks. This may sound exaggerated, but it is true. Ellen's results are a good example and demonstrate the sometimes-stunning transformative power of higher-consciousness healing.

Ellen

Ellen had been suffering from depression, social phobia, and low self-esteem almost all her life. She had been in and out of psychotherapy, counseling, and self-help groups for over fifteen years. Her depression had lessened by the time we met, but she still suffered terribly from her social phobia and low self-esteem. I asked her to measure her suffering on a scale of 0 to 10 (0 being no suffering at all; 10 being utter desperation). Ellen said she was at 7. This meant that she felt strong and painful anxiety every day in many different situations.

Ellen agreed to try higher-consciousness healing and I guided her into relaxation. She chose to see her higher consciousness in the form of a beautiful bright light and she received a purple gem as a healing symbol. Then I encouraged her to visualize her symbol in the middle of her heart and breathe out its good qualities with love first to herself and then to the people she feared. Unfortunately, Ellen was not very optimistic.

"I don't expect instant results," she said seriously.

"Okay," I said. "Just give it a go."

Two weeks later, Ellen and I spoke on the phone.

"My anxiety has decreased from 7 to 1 on the scale," she said, but she still wasn't very impressed. "I definitely feel better," she told me, "but I can't believe it is because of this symbol. I probably feel better because it is the holiday."

"Just try it for another two weeks," I said, smiling inwardly. I had experienced her reaction myself. Sometimes the results of higher-consciousness healing are just too good to believe.

Two weeks later, Ellen came to my office. "Tara," she said, "I am 0 on the scale and I have never been 0 before in all my life. The holiday is over and I even had a terrible argument with my daughter's doctor. Normally, that would have left me shattered. But I am still fine. I am cross with the doctor, but happy with myself." Ellen has remained well. Sometimes, her old fears try to resurface, but when she remembers her healing symbol, she can return to her positive state of mind in a very short time.

. . .

Higher-consciousness healing is based on the principles of Tibetan Buddhism, but the technique itself is new and unique. It can be used by anyone who feels inspired by it, and it will not interfere with the practice of other religious or spiritual beliefs. It is a short and simple method that can be learned and practiced within minutes. Here's how it works:

1. Define your problem—I suffer from feeling (emotion) about (problem)—and rate the strength of your emotion on a scale from 1 to 10. After practicing higher-consciousness healing for two weeks, check how far this number has gone down.

2. Relax and visualize your higher consciousness in a form that pleases you—for example, as a central figure of the religion you follow, as an angelic being, or simply as a shimmering loving light.

3. Ask your higher consciousness for a healing symbol to overcome your problem. With the technique explained in this book, a beautiful, brightly colored symbol will just pop into your mind.

4. Visualize your symbol in your heart and, with every out breath, see how it radiates loving and joyful light toward you and envelops you in a bubble of loving joyful light. The light of your healing symbol will then radiate to everyone who is involved in your problem and envelop them in a bubble of loving joyful light as well. These bubbles of light may touch, but should not merge.

5. Simultaneously, relax the tensions of your negative emotion. Practice in this way for two minutes, twice a day, and every time your negative feeling arises.

Even though higher-consciousness healing is a very simple method, it regularly brings great improvements to even the severest problems. I have worked with clients who were sexually abused as children, and clients who were raped or violently assaulted as adults. I have worked with people who suffered all their lives from panic attacks, addictions, clinical depression, violent anger, chronic pain, and debilitating tiredness. I have also worked with many couples on the brink of divorce, desperate parents, and children suffering from many problems. To my joy, they *all*—with virtually no exception—experienced dramatic and lasting improvements within days or a few weeks by using higher-consciousness healing.

THE HEALING POWER
OF SYMBOLS

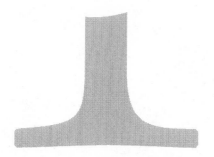

Chapter 1

A Method for Everyone

HIGHER-CONSCIOUSNESS HEALING was developed initially as a method of transpersonal psychotherapy. It was intended for use with emotional problems or relationship issues. As it turns out, however, the method works equally well on problems like addiction, financial worries, physical pain, spiritual blocks, and fatigue. Here are some of the problems you can tackle with higher-consciousness healing:

Anxiety

Depression

Stress

Sadness

Anger

Frustration

Loneliness

Bereavement

Addiction

Alienation

Lack of confidence

Eating disorder

Low self-esteem

Feeling easily dominated
and overwhelmed

Desperation

Feeling traumatized

Feeling weighed down
by responsibility

Grief and hurt

Compulsive behavior

Guilt feelings

Problems in making
decisions

Being too dominant and
controlling

Shock

Problems and stress in
relationships

Physical pain

Weight problems

Exhaustion

Tiredness

Sexual problems

Lack of direction in life

Problems with work
and career

Confusion

Financial problems

Problems in achieving
what you want

Energy blocks

Psychic domination

Being stuck or confused
on a spiritual path

Healing Others

Many, if not most, of our problems involve other people. We may experience difficulties in our relationships or feel victimized by someone who has treated us badly. Higher-consciousness healing *always* has a positive effect on the people involved in our problem, because the core of the practice is altruistic love. Sometimes, higher-consciousness healing has profound effects on these people and changes them in ways that we never thought possible. It is important to note, however, that this influence does not come from our personal mind, with all its little egotistical concerns. It comes from our higher consciousness, which always works in the highest interest of everyone involved. Therefore, higher-consciousness healing will lead us to a solution of our problem that will reduce the suffering of everyone involved in the best and healthiest way possible. The following case study shows these effects quite clearly.

Susan

Susan was married to a man who was verbally abusive to her on a regular basis. I helped her receive a healing symbol from her higher consciousness and showed her how to send love to herself and to her husband by enveloping them both in bubbles of loving joyful light. In her mind, she said to him, "I wish you to be happy" and imagined that if he were happy, he would be very loving. Susan had initially thought that the solution to her marital problem was to become more tolerant toward her husband and to "learn not to be hurt anymore." However, after practicing higher-consciousness healing for a few days, she did something that she had never considered doing before. She told her husband in clear terms that she would leave him if he didn't change his ways. At the same time, she was much kinder to him than before and started to cuddle him for the first time in years. To her joyful surprise, her husband gave up his abusive language and they both started to talk honestly about their feelings. After another three weeks, they were also able to rekindle their sex life. These improvements were stable and lasting.

· · ·

Higher-consciousness healing is an excellent method for helping others in psychological or physical pain. I have seen particularly impressive improvements when parents have used it to alleviate the suffering of their children. Here is an example.

Philippa and Imogen

Imogen, age seven, suffered from extreme shyness—so extreme, in fact, that her teachers suspected she was deaf. Philippa, her mom, transferred Imogen to a Montessori school, but her condition did not improve. Then Philippa learned higher-consciousness healing and started to send love to her daughter with the help of a healing symbol. To Philippa's great surprise, Imogen's shyness dramatically lessened within days of doing this practice. Imogen even started to play with other children—something she had never done before. Imogen's condition continued to improve over the following months.

Healing the Physical Body

Obviously, higher-consciousness healing is not a replacement for any medical treatment. However, I have seen many cases in which it greatly enhanced the effects of good treatment. In particular, it has been very effective in reducing physical pain and chronic tiredness. One of the therapists I trained in the method is a massage therapist. She gave me a long list of well-documented case studies that show how it has helped her clients reduce their various forms of pain. The following case study shows the effectiveness of higher-consciousness healing on the physical body.

Val

Val had suffered from extremely painful menstrual periods for over twenty years. She had tried all kinds of treatment without any lasting success and had resigned herself to the fact that she had to take a handful of strong painkillers every month. She really felt inspired when she heard about higher-consciousness healing and started practicing at once. When she had her next period, she found, to her amazement, that her pain was so reduced that she only needed a single painkiller. Encouraged by this success, she carried on with her visualization and, in the following months, she didn't need any painkillers at all. Since then, Val has stopped her visualizations, but has remained pain-free.

Empowering People to Help Themselves

The best help anyone can offer is to give people an effective tool they can use to solve their problems themselves. Higher-consciousness healing is one such tool. It is a self-help method designed for people looking for an effective way to solve their problems with a minimum of cost, time, and energy. Basically, everyone who feels inspired by this method can work with it.

Higher-consciousness healing is so simple and so safe that most people can learn it easily from this book and practice it on their own without the help of a therapist. Over the years, I have received many grateful e-mails from people who report positive results from this method. Most of the case studies in this book, however, come from my own life-coaching practice, because I was able to monitor these cases more carefully and convince myself that the improvements were real. Here is the story of a man who used higher-consciousness healing all by himself.

Andy

After one of my talks about higher-consciousness healing, a man approached me and told me that he had overcome his depression simply by reading my book and doing the exercise. It was not difficult for Andy to receive his healing symbol—a red ruby—by asking his higher consciousness in relaxation. He then visualized his symbol in his heart whenever a low mood crept up on him. He felt the loving light of his symbol fill his body and mind, and comfort his hopeless spirit. Gradually, he felt better and better. When Andy spoke to me, he had been free of depression for six months.

· · ·

There are very few prerequisites for using higher-consciousness healing. You do not need to be spiritual or religious. It is enough if you can simply trust that there is a part of your mind that is more loving and wise than your everyday self. However, if you are religious or spiritual, you can use your beliefs to practice this method without altering anything about them.

Quite a few people worry that they can't visualize effectively. Fortunately, the kind of visualization you need for this method is so basic that anyone can do it. For example, look at a small object in front of you and study all its details. Now close your eyes and describe the object. If you can do this, you can visualize enough to use higher-consciousness healing effectively. You don't need to "see" everything as clearly as if you were looking at it on television. It is enough to think of your symbol, or just to "know" what it looks like. You can also make a simple drawing of your symbol and look at this image, without visualizing anything at all.

Some people are afraid that higher-consciousness healing may bring up upsetting memories or a healing crisis (things getting worse before they get better). Fortunately, this is not true at all. In all the years that I have been using the method, I have found it to be completely safe and extremely pleasant to practice. In fact, one big advantage of this method is that it will *not* bring up distressing memories or upsetting material.

Higher-consciousness healing is so simple that it can even be used by children (usually from age four onward) and I have regularly seen dramatic improvements in their physical and psychological well-being. It can also be used by parents on behalf of their smaller children.

Thomas

Thomas is the nine-year-old son of one of my clients. His mother taught him the simple practice of higher-consciousness healing. They practiced their respective symbols together each day. Thomas's first symbol aimed at improving his relationship with his stepfather. He was so successful that his stepfather remarked positively on the improvement, even though he didn't know anything about the practice. Then Thomas received a symbol to overcome his shyness at school and promptly felt a lot more confident. His mother told me that Thomas continues to use the method whenever he feels a problem arising—which has been greatly empowering for him.

. . .

Unfortunately, sometimes not everyone wants to solve their problems in such a quick and effective way. In my holistic life-coaching practice, I have found that people can become very attached to their problems. On the surface, they maintain that they want to get better, but in reality, they are much more interested in trying to convince me that their problems are not solvable. Some people even feel offended if you tell them that there is a method that can get rid of their problems in a very short time, and that they don't have to explore their suffering in depth. They react as if you want to take something very precious away from them.

Likewise, some people believe they need to find traumas from their past that have caused their present problems in order to resolve them. If I tell these people this is unnecessary and that their problems can be resolved much faster, some of them are a bit resistant.

Some people remain skeptical even if they experience impressive improvements with higher-consciousness healing. Unfortunately, the rational part of their minds cannot accept the gift that this method really is, and they dismiss its healing power. Others have felt sad after their success with the method. For example, Barbara (whom you met in the introduction) was almost upset after she successfully dissolved her social phobia. She asked, "Why did I have to go through all those years of therapy when it could have been so easy?" I couldn't answer this question, other than to share my feeling that higher-consciousness healing is a wonderful gift that she just hadn't received earlier.

Summary

- Higher-consciousness healing can be used for all personal problems.

- People who are involved in your problem may change in amazing ways, but it is not your personal will that brings about these changes. They are brought about by your higher consciousness, which always acts in the highest interest of everyone concerned.

- Higher-consciousness healing is very effective in reducing physical pain and chronic tiredness.

- Higher-consciousness healing is an effective self-help tool designed for people who want to solve their problems with a minimum of time, money, and energy.

- You do not need to be religious or spiritual to use higher-consciousness healing. You can view your higher consciousness simply as a part of your mind that is more loving and wise than your everyday consciousness.

- Everyone has enough basic visualization skill to use higher-consciousness healing effectively. It is enough to think about your symbol, or simply to know that it is there.

- Higher-consciousness healing is a very straightforward method that is completely free of side effects.

Chapter 2

THE DISCOVERY OF HIGHER-CONSCIOUSNESS HEALING

WHEN I DISCOVERED higher-consciousness healing, I had been suffering for many years from a subtle but deep feeling of emotional hurt and sadness that seemed completely disconnected from what was actually going on in my life. This feeling just would not go away, no matter how much my outer life improved and no matter how much I worked on my inner being with various therapeutic methods and intensive Buddhist meditation. I had tried everything: psychoanalysis, bioenergetics, past-life regression, aroma therapy, crystal therapy, emotional freedom technique, cognitive-behavioral therapy, landmark education, mantra chanting, brain-hemisphere synchronization, and Taoist energy and body work. No matter what I did, the sadness always returned.

I felt very frustrated, but something inside told me that it was possible to solve this problem, just as I had solved many other problems in my life. I fervently wished that my suffering should not be in vain, but that I would be able to use my problem to discover the deepest principles of personal healing in order to help other people. I believe my desire to use my own suffering to help others was one of the reasons my prayer was answered. My own pain has truly been like the grit in an oyster that finally produces a beautiful precious pearl.

During the year that followed my discovery of higher-consciousness healing, I refined the method by using all the knowledge I had gained from my many years of training in Buddhism and psychotherapy.

Sometimes, I had a strange feeling—as if an unseen force were guiding me in this process. For example, my own symptoms sometimes flared up for no clear reason, and this led me to refine the method. After making these adjustments, my symptoms disappeared as quickly as they had come. Over time, higher-consciousness healing brought me a degree of harmony, peace, and happiness that I had never experienced before.

After some of my friends and I had experienced very good results with the method, I felt no hesitation in adding it to my counseling repertoire when working with my clients. In fact, it proved so effective that two things happened. First, I dropped almost all the other techniques I had learned in my Gestalt, family, and body-awareness therapy training in favor of higher-consciousness healing. Second, the length of time my clients spent with me in therapy shortened dramatically, because they often felt "sorted out" after only a few sessions.

Using higher-consciousness healing makes people much more independent, so that they do not need the help of a professional as much—or even at all. Sue, for example, learned quickly to rely on her own inner resources for help.

Sue

Sue contacted me because she wanted to find a partner. She felt lonely, depressed, and very fearful that she would never find someone. We first worked on her fear, which she successfully decreased with the help of a healing symbol. Sue still felt depressed and lonely, however. Therefore, her next symbol focused on her depression and her negative self-talk—"It's just not meant to be" or "It's hopeless." After practicing her new healing symbol for another two weeks, Sue told me that she was able to stop her negative self-talk, and that she felt altogether more positive and trusting. Simultaneously, she went on many blind dates. In the past, she had found blind dates depressing and exhausting, but now she saw them as positive learning experiences. When I last spoke to her, all her depression and fear were gone and her loneliness had been replaced with a faith that she would soon find someone.

Chapter 3

HOW HIGHER-CONSCIOUSNESS HEALING WORKS

A CENTURY AGO, SIGMUND FREUD developed his now famous model of the superego, the ego, and the id. The conscious ego, Freud argued, struggles to keep the antisocial drives of the id and the strict and limiting demands of the moralizing superego at bay.

This model and many of Freud's other theories were hailed as great advances in understanding the human psyche. Many forms of psychotherapy developed after Freud still use his basic ideas to explain how emotional disturbances come about and how they can be cured. Unfortunately, Freud's model of human nature does not give much hope for deeper happiness, because it does not recognize that there is a vast range of potentially positive qualities that lie within each of us that are not part of his model.

The Personality Model

Higher-consciousness healing is based on a model different from Freud's. It has three main parts:

1. The conscious mind (also called the everyday, or personal, mind)

2. The unconscious mind

3. The higher consciousness (also called higher power)

Our conscious mind encompasses everything of which we are aware, including our sense perceptions, feelings, thoughts, and memories. Although some of us like to think that our conscious mind is the largest part of the human mind, it is actually the smallest. Our conscious mind is like the tip of an iceberg, while our unconscious mind is like the large part of the iceberg that lies beneath the water. Our unconscious mind is many times bigger than our conscious mind, because it contains all our past experiences in minute detail, as well as everything we are experiencing at the moment, but of which we may not be aware. This may include background noises that we blank out, or feelings and thoughts we don't want to deal with at the moment. Our unconscious mind is neither negative nor positive in itself. It is more like the storehouse of all the internal and external experiences we have ever had.

Between our conscious and unconscious mind, there is a semipermeable boundary. That means that certain things contained in our conscious mind can become a part of our unconscious, and other things that have been forgotten can become a part of our conscious mind again. If you want to experience this semipermeable boundary in your own mind, try thinking about what you ate yesterday . . . and the day before yesterday . . . and the day before that. If you are like most people, you will not remember what you ate more than two or three days ago. When you can't remember any further back, the boundary between your conscious and unconscious mind has closed. This boundary is the major problem in every kind of psychotherapy that relies on recollecting old traumas in order to heal the patient. I will say more about this problem later, but first, let's explore the role this model of the human mind plays in higher-consciousness healing.

Our Higher Consciousness

By far the biggest part of our mind is our higher consciousness, because it is unlimited and permeates the entire universe, including the minds of every being. In this respect, we cannot talk about our higher consciousness as something personal or individual. It is something we share with every other being in the universe. It is outside of us and something other than what we think we are, yet it is also inside of us and the core of our being. Most of us are unaware of the presence of the higher consciousness, and it is the aim of every genuine spiritual path to make us fully aware of it.

It is difficult to imagine the vastness of our higher consciousness, because it is more than our conscious mind can understand. Also, the notion that we all participate in an all-encompassing mind can seem like an insult to our personal egos, which want to believe that we start and end where our bodies start and end, and that we are separate and highly individual beings.

No matter how hard we try to understand higher consciousness, we cannot fully grasp it because, ultimately, it is a mystery. The idea of something mysterious and all-encompassing is a part of most religions. Christians call it the Holy Spirit; Buddhists call it Buddha-nature. In this book, I call it higher consciousness, so that people of all backgrounds can work with it. And, as I said before, we do not need to be spiritual in order to benefit from higher-consciousness healing.

So what is our higher consciousness like?

Imagine for a moment that you feel utterly free, uplifted, and without limitation. Nothing burdens you; no worries constrict you; joy fills your heart. You feel you have access to unlimited knowledge and infinite possibilities; you are able to do whatever you want. Now imagine that this vast space of freedom is filled with the sweetest and most tender love flowing freely from your heart to all beings without discrimination. All notions of friend and enemy are gone and you can love everyone alike. You can see that other people are suffering and deepest compassion for them springs from your heart. But you can also see the way to happiness with complete clarity and you realize that all the negative ways in which people behave come from their misguided search for happiness. You feel only one deep wish—to remove all the suffering that people are experiencing and show them the path to true happiness.

Can you imagine all this? These feelings and this wisdom will grow stronger as we develop awareness of our higher consciousness. But our higher consciousness is more than I have just described—much more. The love, compassion, and wisdom of higher consciousness is infinite and without boundary. It truly goes beyond the limits of our imagination. Yet it is our true nature—it is what we ultimately are. So how can our higher consciousness help us solve our problems? I have to go back a little bit to explain this.

The Unconscious Mind

You have probably noticed that many problems—and in particular, emotional problems—cannot be solved through merely thinking and talking about them. Obviously, it is nice to let off steam and get some sympathetic support, but this alone will not solve a problem if an essential part of it is unconscious. On the contrary, a problem can seem to get even bigger the more we think and talk about it. It is like zooming in on a problem until nothing else exists in our perspective, but still without finding a solution. Therefore, in order to solve psychological problems, we must find a way to work effectively with the part in us that is causing the problem but is unconscious at the moment. One way of doing this is to enter a psychotherapy program that tries to uncover unconscious material.

Several forms of psychotherapy work on the assumption that emotional or psychosomatic problems are caused by traumatic experiences in the past. These can be in our childhood, or even previous lives. These approaches typically believe that we have to make this traumatic material conscious again in order to release old negative feelings and correct any unhealthy decisions that we made at that time.

Let me illustrate this with an example. A woman who has problems creating committed relationships enters psychotherapy. Through working with her unconscious mind, she is regressed to the age of three and discovers that she was sexually abused. According to the theory, she can now release her suppressed feelings of anger and grief, and thus become happy and successful.

Different therapies use different methods to regress clients and make the unconscious conscious. Unfortunately, bringing up unconscious material can have severe side effects. Regression doesn't acknowledge that there is a very good reason why people relegate terrible traumas from their past to the unconscious. It is one of the most merciful qualities of our mind that it can forget the bad things of our past so readily. If you are over thirty years old, you have probably noticed that your past seems better and better the older you become. This ability to forget many painful things helps us concentrate on our life at the moment and be free of the burdens of our past. People who cannot forget the traumas they have experienced suffer from posttraumatic stress that can make their present a living hell. They actually need help to *forget* the dreadful things they have experienced.

When we dig into our unconscious mind to release old traumas, it can sometimes be utterly devastating. Some people who discover during psychotherapy that they were sexually abused as children report that their recollections are as distressing as if they were being sexually abused again. Instead of releasing old negative emotions, they are swamped and overwhelmed by them.

It is very difficult to deal with recollections like these. They can be extremely painful and can make us feel like a victim. To make matters even worse, there is no way of telling whether these "memories" are true mirrors of reality. Careful investigation of what is actually happening in any form of regression therapy reveals that it uncovers only "pictures in the mind." Nobody can say for sure what these pictures really represent. Are they true recollections? Are they fantasies? Or a mixture of both?

Imagine that you discover in regression that you felt neglected as a baby. What do you do with this "memory"? It is very difficult to go to your mother and ask her about it. In all likelihood, she will be hurt by your questions and deny everything. But one thing is sure—it will make your relationship with your mother much more difficult.

Fortunately, higher-consciousness healing offers a way to deal with the part of our problem that is unconscious in a way that is completely free of risk. With higher-consciousness healing, we do not need to remember any traumas and we do not need to uncover anything that is distressing. It does not matter if the cause of a problem is related to our childhood, or even to a past life. We do not need to know any of that. All this searching for the cause of a problem will make our problem appear bigger, while not solving anything at all.

"But how can we solve a problem," you may ask, "if we don't even know its cause?"

The answer is that knowing the cause of a problem will not necessarily lead us to its solution.

This is where our higher consciousness comes into play. Albert Einstein famously stated, "No problem can be solved from the same level of consciousness that has created it." Einstein here points to the core of higher-consciousness healing. Instead of diving deeply *into* our problems, we need to jump *out* of them by accessing a part of our mind that is more loving and wise than our everyday mind—a part that already knows the solution to our problem—our higher consciousness. Because our higher consciousness penetrates our entire mind, including our unconscious mind, and because it is ultimately wise and loving, it already knows the solutions to all of our problems. If we can access the wisdom of our higher consciousness, we do not need to make unconscious material conscious. We can go for the solution straightaway. And, by the way, once we know the solution to our problem, we often find that we have discovered its cause as well.

How Healing Symbols Work

The big challenge, at this point, is in how we can communicate with our higher consciousness. Most of us only have occasional glimpses of the higher consciousness. Traditionally, meditation and prayer are the only ways to deepen our experience of it. Fortunately, higher-consciousness healing offers a way to communicate with our higher consciousness, even if we have never meditated before.

Language is not well-suited to this communication, because words are much too crude to communicate with higher forms of wisdom and compassion. What we need is something that will bridge the gap between our relatively crude personal mind and our higher consciousness. We can create this bridge with the help of symbols.

The idea of using symbols to communicate with our higher consciousness is not new. Most religions provide symbols that help make this contact. In higher-consciousness healing, we receive our own personal symbols in order to solve our problems. It is important to understand, however, that symbols are more than just little pictures or statues. They are charged with the energy and meaning of what they are meant to communicate, and they really embody what they symbolize. So, in effect, the symbol and what it stands for cannot be separated. They are one.

We can work with symbols in three different ways. First, we can make contact with our higher consciousness by visualizing it in symbolic form. For example, some people choose to see their higher consciousness as a shimmering light or an angelic being; others stick with the well-known images from traditional religions. Second, our higher consciousness can send messages to us in the form of healing symbols. Third, we can focus on these healing symbols in order to send messages deep into our unconscious mind, where information is usually stored in the form of pictures rather than words. This is another reason why language does not work very well in order to solve problems that are rooted deep within our unconscious mind. Using symbols is much more effective and will give our unconscious mind the information it needs to transform.

When we repeatedly give all parts of our mind messages from our higher consciousness in the form of symbols, we can achieve amazing results. New and healthy ideas arise; negative emotional patterns decrease; tiredness disappears. We may also find that our life circumstances begin to change mysteriously. This process is safe, free of side effects, and, most of all, extremely effective. With higher-consciousness healing, we can work on problems that have their roots deep in our unconscious mind without ever getting the undesired side effects that can accompany the uncovering of unconscious material.

"Wait a minute," I can hear you saying. "It can't be that easy! Surely we have to work with our problems at least a little bit!"

You are right. You need to work with your problem—but not in a negative or self-destructive way. Unfortunately, many people think that self-development only works when there is pain, or a crisis, or suffering involved. This is not true. Personal development can be completely free of pain—but only if we have a skillful means of achieving this. What we need is a solution-oriented approach that will create positive feelings, new possibilities, and new insights. Higher-consciousness healing is just such an approach.

Higher-Consciousness Healing Vs. Positive Thinking

Higher-consciousness healing assumes that the root of all problems lies in (unconscious) faulty beliefs about ourselves and about the world. Beliefs like "I am not loveable" or "Women are not trustworthy" create negative emotions and bodily tensions, which, in turn, can lead to neurotic or physical symptoms. Higher-consciousness healing works on the level of these deep beliefs, but in a very different way than traditional forms of positive thinking.

Most forms of positive thinking work by replacing negative beliefs simply by repeating the opposite positive affirmation as often as possible. For example, if we think we are stupid, we need only replace this thought with, "I am intelligent" and repeat it constantly. Unfortunately, negative beliefs will usually not go away that easily. On the contrary, positive thinking can easily degenerate into a constant struggle to keep inner negativity at bay. We may even get on the nerves of our friends, because they quickly sense that our "positiveness" is not that genuine. Unfortunately, by trying too hard to think positively, we often experience even more painful self-denial and separation from others.

Higher-consciousness healing does not use words at all, but simply introduces our inner being to a beautiful *image* that radiates love in all directions. This does not evoke the inner resistance often encountered when we try to *think* positively.

It is, nevertheless, important to stop tormenting ourselves with negative self-talk. Calling ourselves a "fat cow" or a "stupid idiot" will always evoke negative feelings. But your healing symbol can cut through this inner negativity. The following case study shows how this works in practice.

Janice

Janice (who is also a counselor) contacted me because she suffered from depression. Once we had talked about her feelings in more detail, it turned out that she blamed her mother for her depression because she didn't feel properly cared for as a child. Therefore, her first symbol was geared toward resolving her negative relationship with her mother. For two weeks, Janice sent love to herself and her mother every day with the help of a healing symbol. The results were very surprising for Janice, who had been in and out of therapy for decades. Suddenly, she felt more liberated and happy than she ever had before; she felt genuine love for her mother for the first time in years.

However, Janice still suffered from the bad habit of comparing herself unfavorably with others, which made her feel envious and resentful. I talked to her about the importance of stopping this negative self-talk and encouraged her to learn to be her own best friend. From then on, Janice made a great effort to stop her unfavorable comparisons by placing her mind firmly on her symbol and its loving light. As a result, her resentment and envy gradually disappeared.

The Healing Power of Love

The essence of the higher consciousness is love. It is this infinite and unconditional love that radiates out from our healing symbol and produces the often miraculous improvements of higher-consciousness healing. The most important aspect of higher-consciousness healing is to focus on the love that shines forth from our beautiful symbol and allow this love to penetrate all our problems. Love is the sincere wish for ourselves and others to be happy.

> Love is the sincere wish for ourselves and others to be happy.

When we work with a healing symbol, we first let its loving light shine toward ourselves and wish ourselves to be truly happy from the bottom of our heart. Doing this rids us of all forms of self-loathing and raises our self-esteem to a healthy level.

In the next step, we let the loving light of our symbol shine out to all the people who are involved in our problem and wish them happiness as well. It may seem very difficult to send love to the very people who have harmed us, but I have seen that it can be done quite easily when we are supported by a healing symbol from our higher consciousness. Sending love is a positive intention for someone to be happy, rather than a feeling of infatuation or attraction. We do not have to like the person we send love to. Instead, we simply have to imagine that if our adversaries are genuinely happy, they will immediately regret all the bad things they have done and become very likeable people instead. Working in this way has tremendous healing power. Kathy freed herself from the terrible effects of sexual abuse by using this approach.

Kathy

Thirty-two-year-old Kathy had been sexually abused as a child by her uncle. She was full of self-loathing and depression, and hated her uncle with a vengeance. Kathy's biggest problem was that she had never had a single loving encounter with a man, which made her very unhappy. I explained to her that I was optimistic she could find true love, even though she had suffered sexual abuse as a child. In my opinion, her biggest obstacle to finding love was the hatred she felt toward herself and her uncle, not the abuse itself.

Kathy understood what I was trying to say, but she felt that, if she stopped hating her uncle, it would diminish his guilt. I told her that nobody could remove the guilt from her abuser, and that he had to live with it for the rest of his life. "All you have to do," I said, "is to stop hating him. Resentment will tie you to your abuser but love will set you free. Love means to wish your uncle happiness in the knowledge that this will make him into a better person who will regret what he has done intensely. It does not mean that you have to like him or diminish his guilt."

After we had talked all this through, Kathy was willing to give it a try. For the first two weeks, she sent the healing light of her symbol only to herself and experienced a sense of happiness and purity that was completely new and wonderful for her. Then she bravely started to send the light of her healing symbol to her uncle—whom she visualized a very long distance away—and wished him to be happy and loving. As she was doing this, she suddenly had a strong feeling that her uncle had been sexually abused himself as a child, and she even felt a little bit of compassion for him. At that moment, Kathy truly felt free from all the negative effects of the abuse for the first time in her life. Most wonderfully, after practicing in this way for a few weeks and feeling better and better in herself, Kathy happily fell in love for the first time in her life with a very supportive and loving man. In parallel, a chronic pain she had had in her hips simply disappeared.

. . .

Love is the supreme healing power in the universe. We don't need to go back to past traumas to be healed of pain, neglect, and abuse. It is wonderful to see that *all* negative feelings resulting from past trauma can be dissolved effectively by sending love to ourselves and our enemies with the help of a healing symbol. Traumatic experiences themselves do not make us suffer. It is our *current* resentment and victim mentality that causes the pain. When we use the healing power of love, painful emotions subside, physical ailments heal more quickly, and wisdom arises to resolve our conflicts more constructively.

What's more, sending love to others often produces real and positive changes in people we find difficult—even if they don't know anything about our practice. I have seen numerous cases in which people have transformed positively when my clients have sent them love with the help of a healing symbol. Here is another story that demonstrates the power of higher-consciousness healing on others.

Harriet

Harriet had many problems that she blamed on her father—depression, loneliness, and the inability to find a partner. Her father had been in a mental-care home from the time she was a child. Harriet described in elaborate detail how a previous therapist had shown that her current relationship problems were all due to her having grown up with a mentally ill father. "I hate my father," she told me, with tears in her eyes, "he ruined my life." I empathized with Harriet's pain, but I also told her that I believed that it was her **current** resentment toward her father that accounted for her emotional problems and not her childhood experiences in themselves. I then showed her how to send love to herself and her father with the help of a healing symbol. I encouraged her to say to her father in her mind, "I wish you to be happy and healthy."

The effect of this practice was immediate. Harriet felt as if a big burden had fallen off her shoulders; her lifelong feeling of depression virtually disappeared within days. After doing this practice for several weeks, she told me with joy that the mental health of her father had improved so much that he had been able to leave the hospital for the first time in years. She then asked me if I thought this could be due to her practice of higher-consciousness healing. I told her there was no proof of that, but that I wasn't surprised at all, because I had regularly seen similar improvements with higher-consciousness healing. Both Harriet and her father continued to improve.

The Healing Power of Relaxation

Every negative emotion—depression, anger, fear—corresponds to an area in our physical body where tension builds. For example, many people feel depression as a sensation of painful tension in the chest or head; anger often manifests as tension in the legs and arms; anxiety is often felt as a tense knot in the stomach or neck. People tend to have unique, but stable, patterns of tension that go along with their negative emotions. Once we know our personal areas of tension and are able to relax these parts of our body, our negative emotions will be gone. It is as simple as that! Focusing on the loving light of our symbol and letting it penetrate the areas of our bodily tensions make this process very easy and effective.

We can work in exactly the same way with chronic tiredness that cannot be relieved by adequate amounts of sleep. We simply have to notice where in our physical body the fatigue manifests as tension. By patiently releasing these tensions with the help of a healing symbol we can quickly return to a healthy level of vitality.

The Healing Power of Correct Breathing

When we focus on our healing symbol, we let its color radiate out in synchronization with our out breath. The whole focus in higher-consciousness healing is always on the out breath, never on the in breath, because focusing on breathing out makes us more relaxed, while focusing on breathing in makes us more tense. Breathing correctly can thus calm down all sorts of negative emotions and is particularly effective when we work with anxieties and fears. With a healing symbol and the correct form of breathing, we can even alleviate panic attacks in a matter of a few minutes. In my holistic life-coaching practice, I have had many clients who suffered from chronic fear, anxiety, and panic. They all, without exception, were able to free themselves entirely from these negative emotions within a matter of a few days or weeks by focusing on their healing symbols and gently correcting their breathing.

The Healing Power of Visualizing Bubbles of Love

When we send love through higher-consciousness healing, we imagine that this love forms bubbles of loving, joyful light around ourselves and others. These bubbles are roughly as big as our outstretched arms and have a firm boundary. Visualizing these firm boundaries can have a profound effect on our unconscious mind and results in a much greater sense of inner security. It also—almost miraculously—helps clarify difficult relationship entanglements.

Most relationship problems are due to two main dynamics: people are either too submissive and allow themselves to be dominated by others, or they are too egotistical and drive people away through their overbearing behavior. Both problems are due to unhealthy ego boundaries. Self-sacrificing (co-dependent) people give up their own ego boundaries and are unhealthily merged with more dominant people. Typically, these are women. On the other hand, people who are too selfish do not respect the ego boundaries of others and impose their own will on the people around them. Typically, these are men. Most people who seek therapy belong to the first category and have problems with confidence and difficulty saying "no."

In higher-consciousness healing, the healthy ego boundaries of each person are symbolized by firm bubbles of loving, joyful light that emerge from our healing symbol and surround ourselves and others involved in our problem. These two bubbles may touch if we wish, but they should never overlap or merge. A merging of these bubbles symbolizes an unhealthy fusion of people who do not dare assert themselves, or who treat each other in an overbearing way. By repeatedly visualizing beautiful bubbles of loving, joyful light around ourselves and others, we can easily establish healthy ego boundaries, regardless of whether we are a submissive or dominant personality. This can be incredibly powerful, and often restores clarity and love into complex relationship problems in a matter of days or a few weeks. The story of how Gillian's marriage improved, even though her husband knew nothing about higher-consciousness healing illustrates this.

Gillian

Gillian came to see me because she felt she was on the brink of divorce from her husband of sixteen years. She complained bitterly that he had no respect for her and treated her "like a cleaner." When I suggested that she ask her husband to tidy up his stuff, she explained that she was too frightened to do this because he got angry very easily. Her report sounded so negative that I personally doubted her marriage could be rescued. However, after Gillian used a healing symbol to visualize them both within two bubbles of love for two weeks, things improved dramatically. Gillian became able to ask her husband for what she needed and, to her great surprise, he became amenable to her requests. As a result, the atmosphere between the two became quite loving. These improvements continued to deepen and stabilize in the months that followed.

· · ·

I want to mention here that I always work toward preserving a marriage, except in cases of violence and unaddressed addiction. In these cases, I always urge the couple to separate.

The Healing Power of Color

The healing symbol we receive from our higher consciousness needs to have a bright and beautiful color. It is well known that bright colors have a strong effect on our moods and physical well-being. For example, trains are often decorated in soothing blue to stop people from vandalizing them, and newborn babies suffering from jaundice are effectively treated with nothing more than a bright orange light. It is also interesting that in terms of effect, it doesn't make any difference whether the colors are real or imagined.

Higher-consciousness healing uses the healing effect of color by flooding our body and surroundings with the beautiful bright light that radiates from our healing symbol. This further enhances the effectiveness of the method and brings about profound changes in our psychological and physiological well-being.

The Healing Power of Smiling

Higher-consciousness healing is an altogether positive approach that completely dispenses with rummaging through our old traumas and painful emotions. Instead, we go immediately to the solution of our problem, including feeling joyful and happy. Therefore, when we focus on our healing symbol, it is very helpful to jump-start feeling positive by smiling gently. At first, this smile may feel a bit strained, but most people quickly find that it helps them regain a good mood more readily. This is particularly true for those who suffer from sadness and depression. Once they feel better in themselves, they are more able to solve their various problems. The next case study shows how this looks in practice.

Holly

Holly, who is twenty-nine, contacted me because she had suffered from depression all her life. This painful feeling began at the age of ten, when her parents took her to India and she couldn't cope with the sight of abject poverty. In contrast to traditional counseling, I did not ask Holly to relive her painful memories. Instead, I asked her where in her body she felt her sense of depression. After a little introspection, Holly discovered that her depression felt like a black rock in her brain. Then I guided her to send love to herself with the help of a healing symbol and to smile gently to herself. I also asked her to try to "relax the black rock in her brain" by seeing it open like a beautiful flower with every out breath. Within ten minutes, Holly's persistent feeling of depression was gone. However, once she went home, she had difficulty maintaining this happier state. When she came back two weeks later, she reported that her depression was better, but not gone. The "black rock" in her brain now felt like "gray smoke." Once again, I guided her through the process of higher-consciousness healing and, from then on, her depression disappeared completely.

Resolving Negative Emotions

Some people may be concerned that higher-consciousness healing is just a powerful way to suppress negative emotions. Fortunately, this is not at all the case. I have had many opportunities to ask my clients months, even years, after working with them whether they have been able to maintain their improvements. To my joy and delight, virtually everyone reports that their improvements are lasting and stable. What's more, I find no indication that the initial problem has been replaced by different or more severe problems. In general, people are led by higher-consciousness healing to a genuine and healthy solution, and live an altogether better life.

Ron

Ron tried higher-consciousness healing because he had experienced problems in his relationship with his wife for a long time. They both felt dissatisfied and their relationship had been chugging along without any significant highs or lows. When Ron tried my method, he simply expected everything to get better. Instead, however, something happened that was quite unusual for him. He suddenly felt an urge to sit down with his wife and really discuss all the little problems and irritations that had accumulated over the years. And this urge grew stronger and stronger, even though talking about their problems was the very thing that Ron and his wife had avoided throughout their relationship. They had both always been afraid that any kind of argument would mean the end of their marriage. To his astonishment, however, Ron noticed that his fear of discussing problems significantly decreased. So he asked his wife to talk with him and she agreed. Their conversation was not nearly as difficult as Ron had expected, and they found compromises that worked much better than their usual silent, half-grudging arrangements.

...

After all this explanation, you may still be wondering exactly how higher-consciousness healing brings about all these wonderful results. I have to admit that I don't have an answer to this question. The deeper working principles of the method remain inexplicable, as do any other explanations that touch on the primordial ground of our being. The method works by connecting us to the source of deepest love and wisdom in the universe, and this source will always remain a deep mystery. In the same way, the dramatic improvements in well-being that result from the method cannot be explained from a purely rational or psychological point of view. Something much deeper is at work here and we need to value these forces in order to harvest their full results. Therefore, we need to have a little faith in order to give higher-consciousness healing a serious try. Let's get started!

Summary

- Our higher consciousness penetrates our entire unconscious mind and can change our problem at its root. We don't even need to know the cause of our problem.

- In higher-consciousness healing, there is no risk of upsetting or traumatic material coming to the surface as happens in many forms of therapy that work through regression.

- The most effective way to communicate with our higher consciousness and our unconscious mind is through symbols, not words.

- By far the most important aspect of higher-consciousness healing is the love that radiates from our healing symbol—first to ourselves and then to everyone involved in our problem. Loving someone means to wish this person to be happy. It does not mean taking away someone's guilt or liking them. A genuinely happy person would immediately repent all their wrong-doing and become very likeable.

- It is not the actual traumas from our past that make us suffer, but our current resentment and victim mentality. Once these negative attitudes are dissolved with the help of a symbol, we are free to fulfill our dreams.

- Every negative emotion corresponds to an area of tension in our physical body. By learning to relax these tensions the negative emotions will disappear.

- In higher-consciousness healing, we use relaxation, correct breathing, the visualization of bubbles surrounding us, color therapy, and smiling to support the healing process.

HIGHER-CONSCIOUSNESS
HEALING

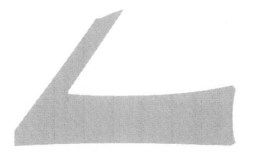

Chapter 4

DEFINING THE PROBLEM

THE FIRST AND MOST IMPORTANT step in higher-consciousness healing is to define our problem precisely and correctly. If the definition of
our problem is broad and vague, the effects of the healing will also be
broad and vague. The more precisely we can point to the core of our
problem, the more effectively the method will work.

When I started to train people as practitioners of higher-consciousness
healing, I found that many of my students were almost addicted to over-
analyzing their problems and trying to find "deeper layers." My clients
often do the same. Many of them try to explain to me all the underlying causes of their problems, to the extent that I start wondering who is
the psychotherapist—them or me. Higher-consciousness healing doesn't
require all this "psychologizing." In fact, too much "deep" analysis of our
problem is not only superfluous, it makes things unnecessarily confusing.
In any case, it is often impossible to know the underlying reasons for our
problems, because they are stored safely away in our unconscious mind.
"Deep" analysis is often no more than guesswork that makes the whole
process vague once more.

Pinpointing Negative Emotions

The core of every problem—no matter how complex and complicated—
is our current negative emotions. Many who come to my life-coaching
practice tell me long stories about all the aspects of their problems. It is
important to talk about all the details of their issues and I always empa-

thize. However, in terms of solving their problems, I only need to know one thing: What is the most painful emotion connected to the problem? Once I know this, I can go straight to helping them receive healing symbols and then letting their higher consciousness do the rest of the work.

Unfortunately, it is easy to get confused when we confront all the intricate aspects of a problem. The best way to clarify is simply to ask: Which negative feeling do I experience most often when I suffer from this problem? Is it mostly like anger, mostly like sadness, or mostly like anxiety?

To get the best results from higher-consciousness healing, we must always work with the emotion that is causing us the most suffering at the moment. For some people, this is very easy; they know very clearly that they are anxious or depressed, for example. However, there are many who are not really in touch with their emotions and who find it difficult to name what they are feeling. For them, the following table can be very helpful. It shows the three main categories of negative emotions: anger, sadness, and anxiety. Virtually all painful emotions belong to one of these categories.

Table 1. Categories of Negative Emotions

Anger (directed at oneself or others)	Sadness	Anxiety
Irritation	Depression	Nervousness
Frustration	Grief	Fear
Impatience	Feeling down	Panic
Boredom	Emotional hurt	Stress
Disgust	Shame	Time pressure
Grudges	Despair	Embarrassment
Revulsion	Emotional pain	Shyness
Resentment		Worry
Bitterness		Phobia
Self-loathing		
Self-hatred		
Hatred		

Feelings like jealousy, envy, and greed belong in one of these categories as well, depending on whether they are a more angry form of this feeling, or a more anxious or sad form. For example, in greed, either anxiety (to miss out) or anger (about having missed out) can be the most predominant feeling.

> We must always work with the emotion that is causing us the most suffering.

If we find it difficult to pinpoint our negative emotion, we can ask ourselves whether our negative feeling is most like anger, most like sadness, or most like anxiety. Knowing the main category of our feeling is usually enough to get good results with higher-consciousness healing. If we suffer from stress at work, for instance, it is not enough to define our problem simply as stress. Is our stress mostly like anger, like sadness, or like anxiety? Once we know our negative feeling, we should define our problem in exactly the following form:

I suffer from feeling (emotion) about (problem).

The exact definition of our problem is important in order to receive clear feedback later on. Let me give you an example. If we are one of the many people who suffer from being overweight and who want to shed some pounds, it is not enough to define our problem simply as "suffering from being overweight." If we want to use higher-consciousness healing for this problem, we need to ask ourselves: What exactly do I feel when I experience the suffering from being overweight? Is my feeling mostly like anger, sadness, or anxiety? Not everyone feels the same negative emotions about the same problem. Some may be depressed about their weight (sadness category), while others may be very frustrated (anger category). If we feel emotions from two categories (for example, self-loathing and fear), we need to decide which of these feelings is the more painful and work with the strongest emotion first. For example, if self-disgust (anger category) is our worst emotion, we may define our problem like this: I suffer from feeling disgusted about my body.

If we have a problem that involves many different emotions (like a divorce, for example), always start with the most painful one. Later, we can work through the different layers of emotion with different symbols. (See chapter 13 for how to work through complex problems.)

Sometimes, people tell me they are not suffering from negative emotions, but they have an unfulfilled wish. If they only had a partner or a job, they would be happy. However, in every situation where we feel unhappy, we can also find negative emotions. If we wish for a partner, for example, we may be suffering from feeling sad or frustrated. If we are unemployed, we may be suffering from feeling worried or depressed. When we use higher-consciousness healing for problems like these, we may not get a job or a partner right away, but we will definitely feel better in a genuine way. Once we feel happier, we will also be more successful in our search for whatever we desire. (See chapter 17 for more details on wish fulfillment.)

If we suffer from physical pain or fatigue, we can simply name our problem as "suffering from feeling pain" or "suffering from feeling tired." Pain and fatigue are obviously not emotions, but defining our problem in this way will work well.

The Body-Mind Connection

Once we have named our negative feeling, we need to explore where our emotion manifests in our physical body. All feelings always have a physical aspect that manifests as tension in various parts of our body. Knowing our unique pattern of tensing up will help us dissolve our disturbing feeling more effectively later on in the process.

For some people, the body-mind connection is very obvious; they know immediately that their anxiety feels like a big knot in their solar plexus, for example. However, for some, emotional tension is a new concept and they need some support to find the physical manifestation of their emotions. As a general guideline, anger often manifests in the arms and legs, sadness or depression can often be felt in the chest, eyes, or head, and anxiety can often be felt in the solar plexus, throat, and shoulders. However, it is important that you find your personal pattern of emotional tension in your own body. Here is a little exercise to help you.

1. For a short moment, think of your problem and feel the main negative emotion that is associated with it (anger, sadness, or anxiety). Once you feel the negative feeling, ask yourself: Where in my body do I feel this negative feeling?

2. Don't worry if you can't answer this question immediately. Instead, scan your body in search of your negative feeling. Start with your toes. Is the negative feeling in your toes? In your feet? In your ankles, knees, thighs, abdomen? Is it around your waist, in your chest, or in your shoulders, arms, hands, neck, face, eyes, or head?

3. If you suffer from fatigue, do the same exercise and look closely to find where in your body your sense of tiredness manifests itself.

Once we know where in our body we feel our painful emotion, we can relax again and continue with the process of higher-consciousness healing. We will come back to these emotional tensions later in order to dissolve them.

Defining Our Problem Correctly

Once we have named our negative emotion and explored its mind-body connection, we can define our problem in the following format:

I suffer from feeling (emotion) about (problem).

In my many years of working with higher-consciousness healing, I have found that this form of problem definition brings the best results. And once we have clear feedback that the method works for us, we will be motivated to carry on with this approach. Table 2 provides some examples of correct and incorrect problem definition.

Sometimes, people feel anxious or depressed about nothing in particular. If we experience this form of free-floating negative emotion, we can simply define our problem like this: I suffer from feeling sad/anxious/irritable.

Table 2. Correct and Incorrect Problem Definition

Correct	Incorrect
I suffer from feeling afraid of my boss.	I suffer from stress at work (too vague).
I suffer from feeling frustrated about my weight.	I suffer from feeling fat ("fat" is not an emotion).
I suffer from feeling sad about not having a girlfriend.	I suffer because I had a neglectful childhood and this is why I feel lonely now (overanalysis).
I suffer from feeling frustrated about not having enough money.	I suffer from having no money (no emotion).
I suffer from feeling grief about the death of my mother.	I want to be happy again. (This is a wish.)
I suffer from feeling angry about the arguments with my husband.	I suffer from my husband's temper. (We need to discover our own emotion.)
I suffer from feeling frustrated because I don't know which career to pursue.	I suffer because I haven't found my dream job yet (no emotion).
I suffer from feeling depressed. (If there is nothing specific about which we feel depressed we can define our problem in this short way.)	I suffer because I was abused (no emotion).
I suffer from feeling the pain of sciatica.	I suffer from feeling stress that has led to the sciatic pain (overanalysis).

In some cases, people worry that higher-consciousness healing may help them get rid of their negative emotions but not solve their problems. This worry is unfounded, as the following case study demonstrates.

Jane

Jane came to see me because she was depressed about her nonexistent career. When I helped her to define her problem, she said that it was more important for her to find a job than it was simply to feel better. My answer was that if she were happier, she would be much more able to solve her problems. Jane, for example, was so depressed that she couldn't even get out of bed in the morning. Therefore, we defined her problem like this: I suffer from feeling depressed about my career. She received a purple gemstone as a healing symbol, which helped her decrease her depression substantially. Once she felt better, she was able to go to the job center, write applications, and cope with rejections.

Summary

- The most important aspect of the problem definition is the current negative emotion associated with your problem.

- There are three main categories of negative emotions: anger, sadness, and anxiety. Try to pinpoint which of these you feel when you experience your problem.

- Explore where in your body you can sense your negative emotion or sense of fatigue. Knowing this will help you dissolve your feeling later.

- Define your problem in the following way: I suffer from feeling (emotion) about (problem). Don't try to guess what the underlying cause may be.

Chapter 5

MEASURING OUR SUFFERING

IN THE NEXT STEP, we measure our negative emotion associated with our problem on a scale from 1 to 10. Several forms of psychotherapy measure negative emotions quantitatively and it is a powerful tool. In higher-consciousness healing, we do it to get feedback on the results of the method. I have often seen people forget how bad their problems had been after only two weeks of practicing the method. Unfortunately, this can lead them to dismiss the method's effectiveness. When they get proper feedback by measuring their negative emotions on a scale, however, it increases their motivation to carry on. The following story illustrates this point.

Zoe

In one of my talks, I guided everyone through the practice of higher-consciousness healing. The whole group relaxed, made contact with their higher consciousness, and received healing symbols. Then I told them all how to visualize their healing symbols over the next two weeks. Zoe phoned me two weeks later about something that had nothing to do with the method. After we had talked about this, I asked her how she was getting on with her healing symbol. She told me that she had asked for a symbol to overcome her suffering from grief about her brother, who had died recently. She admitted that she hadn't practiced her healing symbol for the required two-week period, and that she had stopped as soon as she felt better. I reassured her that I didn't mind at all, and asked her whether she could remember what her grief had measured on the scale on the evening of my talk. There was silence at the other end of the telephone for a moment. Then Zoe said,

"Tara, I can't believe that I was suffering so much. I had completely forgotten how bad it was only two weeks ago. When I was at your talk, I felt that my grief measured 8 on the scale. My whole life felt like one big trauma. I feel so much better now. I would say my grief is no more than a 3 on the scale."

. . .

When you rate your suffering on a scale, remember to rate only your negative emotion and not "the whole problem." For example, if you have defined your problem as suffering from feeling depressed about your weight, rate the amount of your depression and not the amount of your weight loss. Dissolving our negative emotions is the most important aspect of higher-consciousness healing, because, once we feel happier, we will be much better at doing whatever we want to do—including losing weight. The following list explains each number on the scale in more detail.

0: We do not experience any negative emotion at all. At 0, we don't have a problem.

1: We feel a very slight negative emotion, which hardly bothers us at all.

2: Our negative emotion comes up every now and then, but we can still ignore it most of the time quite easily.

3: Our negative emotion is hard to ignore any more. We are still happy most of the time, but we feel we have to do something to solve our problem.

4: We suffer a good deal from our negative emotion, although we can still switch off from our problem.

5: Our negative emotion is so strong that it gives us a considerable amount of suffering, and switching off becomes quite hard.

6: Switching off from our negative emotion becomes harder and harder. It bothers us most of the time and causes us a lot of suffering.

7: We are starting to get desperate.

8: We are deeply unhappy. We experience almost nothing else but our negative emotion and we have very little hope left.

9: We are extremely desperate. We are completely engulfed by our negative emotion and we have lost all hope.

10: We are completely and utterly desperate.

Some people make huge leaps down the scale of suffering within a few days of starting to use higher-consciousness healing. However, most can expect substantial results after two weeks of practice (at least 2 or 3 points down the scale). This is why I advise people to practice the method for at least two weeks and then measure their suffering on the scale and compare the results. Most people improve even more after another two to four weeks even though they may also experience some smaller ups and downs within this time span. Four to six weeks is an extremely short time for getting rid of a lifetime of neurotic symptoms, but some people have a tendency to stop any method that doesn't bring instant and complete results. In cases like these, it is very helpful to use numbers as an encouragement to keep going.

In some cases, people find it difficult to think about their emotions quantitatively. This is understandable, because our emotions come from the right half of our brain, while our ability to think logically in numbers comes from the left half. It is not always easy to get the two hemispheres to work together. However, the more they are in harmony the more effective and successful we can be as a whole person. When we don't have different compartments for our emotional, intuitive, and creative concepts on the one hand and our rational, analytical, and logical concepts on the other, we can respond to every situation emotionally and rationally at the same time. Using numbers to measure our negative emotions is one way to train ourselves to make our two brain hemispheres work together. It brings rational awareness to more emotional people, and emotional awareness to people who are more rational.

Summary

- Measure how much you suffer from your negative emotion on a scale of 0 to 10, where 0 is no suffering at all and 10 is utter desperation. Only measure your negative emotion and not the "whole problem."

- Measure your suffering again after you have practiced higher-consciousness healing for two weeks and compare the results.

- Having a clear feedback system will enhance your motivation and encourage you to carry on.

Chapter 6

RELAXING OUR BODY AND MIND

ONCE WE HAVE DEFINED our problem and measured our negative emotions on a scale, we are ready to start in earnest. In order to receive a healing symbol, we must contact our infinitely loving and wise higher consciousness—the core of our being, our true nature, and the true nature of the whole universe. Unfortunately, we are rarely fully in contact with our higher consciousness. Those who are fully at one with their higher consciousness have truly transcended the human world—yet they will be all the more human for it, more humble and more compassionate than anyone else. They will be full of inspiring humor and have the deep wisdom to help others. Our higher consciousness is simultaneously the crown of human development and the way we transcend it. Why, then, is it so difficult to be more fully in contact with our higher consciousness? Why, if it is our true nature, can't we be more aware of it?

The biggest hindrance to recognizing our higher consciousness is fear—a very deep and basic fear that we all carry around with us, even if we are not aware of it. It is this fear that motivates most of our thoughts and actions, and fuels our constant questions: How can I get what I want? Am I being supported? How can I get rid of the things I don't like? How can I stop being invaded and controlled by others? We may not be very conscious of these questions, nor of the fear that lies behind them, but they control how we tackle most of the situations in our life.

When we are in complete union with our higher consciousness, all these questions cease to exist and we can be completely trusting. There is nothing but a constant flow of love and joy and a natural wisdom that enables us to do whatever is beneficial for all. When we are in contact with our higher consciousness, we are so happy that we have energy and genuine concern for others—naturally and effortlessly.

When we become more aware of our higher consciousness, we also develop more confidence in ourselves. This is not the same confidence we see in arrogant and self-centered people. True confidence makes our heart open and compassionate, and makes us very modest in a happy way. When we lose our basic fears, we don't need to think about ourselves the whole time. It genuinely doesn't matter as much how we look, how much money we earn, or what others think of us. We are just too happy to be bothered about questions like this. The challenge is to overcome our deep fears and get closer to our higher consciousness.

The best antidote to fear is relaxation. In fact, it is impossible to experience fear in a deeply relaxed state, because fear is nothing other than tension. You have probably noticed how tense your body becomes when you are really afraid—how your breathing becomes fast and shallow, and how your mind can't stop thinking about the very thing that is making you afraid. If you can lie down, relax your whole body, practice slow breathing, and let go of the stressful inner images, your anxiety disappears within minutes.

In order to work with higher-consciousness healing, we do not need to be able to relax very deeply. For most people, a little bit of relaxation is quite enough and can be achieved by going through one of the suggested relaxation methods.

Some people have a relaxed body, but a very tense mind; others have a relaxed body and a sleepy mind. Neither state is desirable for higher-consciousness healing. The ideal to aim at is a relaxed body and a calm, but alert, mind.

If you have practiced relaxation exercises before, you can use whatever method suits you best. In the overview of higher-consciousness healing at the end of the book, there is a reliable and effective method you can try. If you find that this form of relaxation doesn't work for you, here are two alternative methods:

1. Sit or lie down comfortably and undo any belts or tight clothing.

2. Let yourself become aware of the rhythm of your breathing. Imagine you are sitting on a sled and, every time you breathe out, you slide down a gentle, snowy mountain slope. As your out breath finishes, your sled comes to a gentle standstill at the bottom of the hill. Be aware of the time that elapses before you begin to breathe in. Allow this gap to lengthen for as long as is comfortable. Then gently breathe in and see yourself sliding down the gentle mountain slope again as you breathe out. Gently lengthen the gap at the end of your out breath. Carry on breathing like this for a few moments.

3. Tense the muscles in your feet as you breathe in, and when you breathe out, release all the tension in your feet. Tense the muscles of your calves and then release them with your next out breath. Continue this pattern as you tense and then release the muscles of your thighs, stomach, chest, shoulders, arms, hands, neck, face, and head.

4. Imagine you are sitting on a beautiful cloud, sailing gently toward a wonderful place of your choosing—a beach or a garden. When you arrive at this beautiful place, climb off your cloud and sit or lie down somewhere where you feel comfortable.

5. Enjoy your deep relaxation.

If this breathing method doesn't work for you, try this visualization exercise:

1. Sit or lie down comfortably and undo any belts or tight clothing.

2. Feel your right leg becoming more and more relaxed. Feel your left leg becoming more and more relaxed. Your right arm becomes more and more relaxed and so does your left arm. Your whole body becomes more and more relaxed.

3. Now your right leg becomes comfortably warm. Your left leg becomes comfortably warm. Your right arm becomes comfortably warm and

so does your left arm. Finally, your whole body becomes comfortably warm.

4. See yourself drifting through an endless open space. You feel wonderful in this space. You are surrounded by love and happiness and you feel free and liberated.

5. Now you see a beautiful bright light in the distance. You feel drawn to this light and you move nearer and nearer to it. Finally, you enter the radiant light and it surrounds you with pure love. You merge with this light and then move through it. When you've passed through the light, you find yourself in a beautiful place. It may be a garden or a beach or a beautiful house.

6. Find a place to sit or lie down comfortably and enjoy your relaxation.

In some cases, higher-consciousness healing can produce results that resemble miracles. I am reluctant to take any credit for these "miracles"; I am just deeply grateful that they occur. The next case study demonstrates a miraculous improvement in the health of a ten-year-old boy.

Amy and Harry

Amy, the mother of ten-year-old Harry, contacted me deeply concerned that her son was seriously ill with colitis (chronic inflammation of the large intestine). He had stopped growing and, at the time, his condition was so severe that he was hospitalized and being fed through a nose tube. I helped Amy receive a healing symbol on behalf of her son—an image of an angelic being in a long white robe. Amy was very happy about this symbol. She went home and showed her own mother and her husband how to practice higher-consciousness healing, and they all visualized the angelic being in Harry's heart radiating with love. To their great delight, the boy made such a quick recovery that it stunned his doctors. After a very short time, he was allowed to leave the hospital and go to school. A little later, his parents found a new and side-effect-free medication that improved his health even further.

Summary

- The biggest obstacle to making contact with your higher consciousness is a basic fear that everyone carries around with them.

- A relaxed body and a calm, but alert mind will help you experience more of your higher consciousness and receive healing symbols.

Chapter 7

CONTACTING OUR HIGHER CONSCIOUSNESS

OUR HIGHER CONSCIOUSNESS is the nature of the universe, and also the nature of ourselves. In its essence, it is infinite space imbued with love, wisdom, and bliss. For most people, it is easiest to visualize it in a personified form like an angelic being that is infinitely loving and wise. Doing this is probably not very difficult for people who hold religious beliefs. In order to practice higher-consciousness healing they can simply visualize a central figure of their religion and open their hearts to this divine being.

Those who do not have any spiritual beliefs can think of their higher consciousness as the part of their mind that is more loving, happy, and wise than they feel at the moment. They may choose to see it simply as shimmering light. In fact, we can choose to visualize higher consciousness in whatever form is inspiring for us—for example, as an angelic being, a wise old man, or a living and loving light—as long as our inner image is really beautiful.

In my counseling practice, I have found that there is only one form of visualization that doesn't work well: imagining that our higher consciousness looks like ourselves. Even though our higher consciousness is the essence of ourselves, we tend to miss its vast power when we visualize it as looking like us.

You may ask how our higher consciousness can take all these different forms. The answer is that we always perceive it from our personal point of view, depending on our culture, belief system, upbringing, and religious background. This personal context determines both the way we perceive the world and the way we perceive our higher consciousness. There is nothing wrong with this and higher-consciousness healing will work no matter what form we give to our higher power. However, even though our higher consciousness can appear in many forms that are dependent on our own perspective, we don't "own" it. We all share higher consciousness, because it is the nature of the universe.

In order for higher-consciousness healing to work, we do not have to have a mystical vision of our higher power. Therefore, if our higher consciousness doesn't appear spontaneously in front of our inner eye, we can simply choose how we want to imagine it. For example, many of my clients like to perceive it as a shimmering light that has a living and deeply loving quality. It is important always to visualize your higher consciousness in a beautiful color and surrounded by brilliant radiant light.

> Visualize your higher consciousness in a beautiful color, surrounded by radiant light.

No matter how we perceive our higher consciousness, remember that it is always wise and loving, and never critical or judgmental. If our higher consciousness seems to be criticizing us or anyone else, the channel to our higher power is blocked. The critical voice we hear is actually the voice of our own personal consciousness. If this happens, we simply need to relax a little more and try again.

How do we know if we are perceiving our higher consciousness correctly and not just making it up? The answer is that we will always perceive a mixture of our higher consciousness and our own personal consciousness. On a "good day," we will perceive more of our higher consciousness; on a "less good day," we may perceive more of our personal consciousness. This is quite normal and does not decrease the effectiveness of higher-consciousness healing. In order to use this method, we don't need to be an advanced spiritual seeker. All we need is to have the wish to open up to our higher consciousness. At the end of the day, the only thing that matters is that higher-consciousness healing brings results in a straightforward way.

Once we are in contact with our higher consciousness, we need to ask for help. Asking for help can be difficult for some, because it means admitting that we are not as strong and self-reliant as we would like to be. But, in order to gain the full benefit of our higher consciousness, we have to give up the idea that we are completely autonomous and in control. Even though our higher consciousness is the essence of ourselves, we need to perceive it as something higher and stronger than ourselves because, otherwise, we can't really open up to its enormous power. The help of our higher consciousness is the most beautiful gift in the universe, and we need some humility in order to receive it gratefully.

Alison

Alison contacted me because she felt very lonely and depressed. Her most painful emotion was sadness and she received a healing symbol to overcome this feeling. I showed Alison how to send love to herself with the help of her healing symbol and envelope herself in a comfort blanket made of its loving light. At first, she found this hard and recognized that she had the irrational idea that she deserved to be punished. She immediately wanted to find out where this belief came from, and started to blame her neglectful mother. I discouraged Alison from doing this, however. Instead, I explained to her that no one can be sure where their irrational ideas come from, and that blaming her mother would only make matters worse. Once she accepted this line of thinking, I instructed her to send the loving light of her symbol to herself and to her mother, and to wish her mother to be happy from the bottom of her heart. When Alison came back after two weeks, she reported that all her sadness was gone and that she had had the best conversation with her mother in years. Subsequently, Alison started to make more contact with other people and continued to feel much happier than before. Her sadness and her neurotic beliefs about deserving to be punished simply disappeared.

Summary

- People who do not have any spiritual beliefs can think of their higher consciousness as the part of the mind that is more loving, happy, and wise than they feel at the moment.

- You do not need to have a mystical vision of your higher power in order for higher-consciousness healing to be effective. You can simply choose how you want to perceive your higher power—for example, as a central figure of your religion, as a beautiful angelic being, or simply as a shimmering light.

- Even though we may use different images for our higher consciousness, we always share it with all beings in the universe.

- Your higher consciousness is always beautiful, wise, and loving. If it seems ugly, judgmental, or critical, you are actually perceiving your personal consciousness.

Chapter 8

EXPLORING OUR LIFE-PATH

EXPLORING OUR LIFE-PATH is not an essential part of higher-consciousness healing. It simply allows us to understand ourselves more deeply and receive additional feedback. Therefore, you can skip this part of the practice if you wish.

In order to explore our life-path, we imagine our higher consciousness sitting on top of a mountain. As I have said before, we don't need to "see" a clear picture when we visualize this. It is enough to have an idea of the mountain and of our higher consciousness. Then we ask our higher consciousness to show us a road, a path, or a track leading up the mountain. This image of a path, which symbolizes our life-path, will just "pop" into our mind. It is our personal route toward our highest unfoldment.

We all lead different kinds of lives. One person is a computer consultant; another is a teacher or a housewife. Whether the life we have chosen makes us happy depends on one fact alone—whether it brings us nearer to our higher consciousness. This journey is symbolized by the path that leads toward our higher consciousness on top of the mountain. There are as many different roads toward higher consciousness as there are beings. No one needs to develop in exactly the same way as anyone else, and we are all free to find the path that exactly suits our needs and talents. *What* we are doing is not the most important factor. What counts is our *motivation* for doing it.

When we walk up our life-path and finally unite with our higher consciousness, we realize the love and compassion for all beings that is dormant within ourselves. On this journey, we become truly and deeply happy and gain the liberating wisdom that teaches us the true nature of the universe. And we also help others to realize the happiness we've found for ourselves.

The image of the life-path that pops into our mind is different for everyone. For some, it is a wide paved road; for others, it is a steep rocky path. Most see it as having different sections that represent the more or less difficult phases in their lives.

Once we have received an image of our life-path from our higher consciousness, we need to express our gratitude. Every time we acknowledge the help we receive, we become more open and receptive. And the more open we are, the more we will receive the full benefit of this work.

Receiving Answers from Our Higher Consciousness

Unfortunately, there is not much that distinguishes messages from our higher consciousness from our other thought processes. These messages may come into our mind as thoughts or images accompanied by feelings and body sensations. Unfortunately, even if these images and ideas feel great, there is no guarantee that they are channeled exclusively from our higher consciousness. It is important to be realistic about this so we don't fall into the trap of a spiritual "ego-trip." We should take whatever comes into our mind with a pinch of salt and see if it makes sense to us. What matters is whether we can learn something from the images we receive. A helpful message from our higher consciousness will feel good and it is often accompanied by a sense of relief.

Most people find it fairly easy to receive messages from their higher consciousness, but sometimes they get a feeling that the images they receive are their own fantasies, or even pure nonsense. If you feel like this, ask your higher consciousness again. Watch out for an inner feeling of relief or relaxation, or for a little sigh. These are all signs that you are on the right track. If you feel uncomfortable with your message, it is very likely that your inner image has come from your personal consciousness. If that is the case, go back to your relaxation and try again.

It is not a good idea to ask our higher consciousness the same question more than two or three times in a row, because the part of our mind that receives answers on an intuitive level tires quickly. It is better to give ourselves a break after two or three attempts and try again later. With practice, our intuition will sharpen and we will find it easier to receive messages from our higher consciousness. What is important is not to give up too soon.

Sometimes, people say that they don't get a response at all when they ask their higher consciousness a question. In most cases, this isn't true. Many people actually do get an inner picture or thought, but they quickly dismiss it. Unfortunately, by doing that, they shift their state of mind and are less connected to their higher consciousness. If you find that you are not getting any answers from your higher consciousness, check whether you have dismissed the very first (and perhaps shadowy) thought that came into your mind immediately after you asked your question.

The Imagery of the Life-Path

Now we ask our higher consciousness to show us where we are on our life-path. We may get a picture or an idea of ourselves standing down in the valley, or we may see ourselves already near the top of the mountain. It really doesn't matter where we are on the path. What matters is that we are moving forward. As long as we are walking in the right direction, we will be happy—whether we are still in the valley or already near the top. We will be happy because we are fulfilling the purpose of our life—moving closer to our higher consciousness.

The first time I asked to be shown my life-path, I saw a huge mountain. It had a rocky slope near the top that only an experienced rock climber would be able to climb. In the middle, there was a steep stony path; near the bottom was a fairly flat, wide road. I saw myself on this road down in the valley. I was pleased with this image, because I liked the prospect of a flat easy road for a while.

Our life-path represents the path of our personal and spiritual growth. It shows the shortest and most harmonious way to develop our full potential. We are all different; what works for one person may not work for another. This is as true for learning a new language as it is for developing our personal and spiritual potential. If we see several paths leading up the mountain, it is always the shortest one that will bring us the deepest happiness.

We are completely free to decide whether we want to follow our life-path. This means we can choose for ourselves whether we want to grow personally and spiritually. No one can force us to climb up the mountain and develop our potential. Not even our higher consciousness can do that. On the other hand, nobody and nothing can stop us if we decide we want to move closer to our higher-consciousness.

So the obvious question is: How can we be sure we are following our life-path? The answer is that in order to move along our life-path, we must develop a compassionate heart and a wise mind, no matter what is happening to us. By contrast, if we become bitter or depressed and allow ourselves to be controlled by others, our progress on our life-path will be slow. On our life-path, there are no problems—only challenges we are happy to overcome. On our life-path, we may experience adversity, but we will know how to turn problems into wisdom and compassion. For example, if we feel rejected and harmed by others, following our life-path means developing extraordinary compassion instead of becoming resentful and depressed. If we are ill, following our life-path means finding a way to use this illness for personal growth instead of becoming full of self-pity.

Please don't think that suffering is something bad, or a sign that you are failing in your development. On the contrary, for most of us, suffering is the only thing that will turn us again and again toward a concern for our inner growth. Without problems, most of us would never dream of following a path of self-development that involves effort and discipline. Only through admitting to our suffering can we use it to progress along our life-path more happily.

Therefore, the next question we must ask our higher consciousness is what we are doing on our life-path when we experience our suffering from our problem. For example, we may receive images of walking slowly and with effort. We are even more likely to see ourselves standing still, sitting down, moving backward, or even moving along other paths that lead us away from our higher consciousness. When we ask this question, we should go back to our initial definition of our problem (see chapter 4) and ask in the following way:

Please show me what I am doing on my life-path when I suffer from feeling (emotion) about (problem).

Here are two examples of answers my clients have received to this question:

- Rob suffered from worries about money. When he asked his higher consciousness what he was doing on his life-path when he was suffering from feeling worried about his financial situation, he saw himself crouching down and feeling tense.

- Claire suffered from a major problem in her relationship with her boyfriend. When she asked her higher consciousness what she was doing on her life-path when she felt angry with her boyfriend, she saw herself walking along a different path that led away from her higher consciousness.

Most people readily get inner pictures or ideas when they ask what they are doing on their life-paths when they are experiencing their problems. To most, these images make immediate sense. When we are confronted with the truth, it is as if something clicks into place. Pictures are like clues that can give us a general idea of what is going on. For example, Claire realized in a flash that if she carried on in the same way with her boyfriend, she would become more and more unhappy.

Again, please don't judge yourself if you find that you are not walking happily along your life-path. Instead, see this information as the first step to improving your life. After all, if we don't know that we have lost our life-path, we can't do anything to come back to it again. The following list gives a rough guideline of how to interpret the imagery of the life-path. It is intended only as a guide, however. Please feel free to interpret your life-path in the way that feels true to *you*.

- A steep path in front of us: The next phase of our development will be hard work, but very rewarding.

- A flat path in front of us: The next phase of our development will be easy.

- A fork in the path: There is a possibility that lures us away from our original path.

- We can only see bits of our life-path: We do not see our life's purpose.

- Our path disappears behind the back of the mountain: We don't know how we want our life to unfold.

- The path seems to disappear altogether: We feel confused and without direction.

- There is a river crossing our path: We are experiencing obstacles.

- There are big rocks on our path: We are experiencing obstacles.

- Our path is muddy or covered with little rocks : We are experiencing many small obstacles.

- Our path is smooth: We do not experience any obstacles.

- We are in a dark forest: Depends what a dark forest means to us—it could mean we feel hopeless and trapped, or we feel surrounded by protective forces.

- We walk through bleak and rocky terrain: Our life feels barren and hard.

- We walk through a beautiful landscape: Our life feels beautiful and harmonious.

- The weather is sunny/rainy/gray: Our emotional landscape is happy/sad/joyless.

- We are looking downhill instead of uphill: We are looking away from the solution of our problem.

- We are standing still: We do not actively work for the solution of our problem.

- We are sitting down: We feel hopeless or confused, or we are lazy.

- We are walking downhill: We are actively moving away from the solution of our problem.

- We are walking parallel to our path through difficult terrain: We are making it unnecessarily hard for ourselves.

- We are walking on another path, away from our original path: We have lost our life's purpose.

- We move forward, but very slowly: We are going in the right direction, but we are making it unnecessarily hard for ourselves.

- We are moving back and forth: We are undecided.

- We tread on one spot: The way we are trying to solve our problem is fruitless.

- We move forward at a good speed: We are solving our problem in the best way possible.

The following case study shows how the imagery of the life-path can give us feedback on our progress.

Roger

Roger contacted me because he had lost his job and was unable to find another. He was beside himself with anxiety. Roger was an atheist and chose to see his higher consciousness as a shimmering light. He was shown his life-path as a steep rocky road and saw himself as halfway up the mountain, confronted by a torrential stream that blocked his way. When Roger asked his higher consciousness what he was doing on his life-path when he suffered from fear about his work situation, he saw himself walking nervously back and forth along the stream. All this made perfect sense to him, because it mirrored his anxiety and indecision. He then received a healing symbol—a golden star—and he worked with it for two weeks. When he came back to me, Roger reported that he felt much calmer and had been able to think more rationally about his problem. He had even started to consider new career possibilities. I guided him into relaxation and instructed him to ask his higher consciousness what he was doing on his life-path. To Roger's surprise, he discovered that a bridge had appeared across the wild river and he saw himself walking slowly over the bridge. This image reassured him that he was on the "right" path. In the following weeks and months, he started his own business with the help of a friend and the imagery on his life-path "improved" simultaneously. Obviously, Roger felt a lot better as well.

• • •

This case study shows how we can check the imagery of our life-path again and again to receive feedback from our higher consciousness on our progress. In the many years that I have been working with my clients with this imagery, I am still surprised how accurate it is. Only very rarely do people receive images that do not make sense to them. If this happens to you, feel free to dismiss these images, as they are not essential for higher-consciousness healing to work.

Summary

- Working with the life-path imagery is not essential for higher-consciousness healing. You can skip it if you experience problems with it.

- Your life-path is the path of your own personal and spiritual development; it leads toward your higher consciousness. It is your own choice whether you follow it or not.

- Ask your higher consciousness to show you your life-path and where you are on it at the moment.

- Messages from your higher consciousness come into your mind as images or thoughts accompanied by feelings or bodily sensations. If you are not sure whether you have received a genuine message from your higher consciousness, ask again. Feelings of well-being and relief are signs that you are on the right track.

- Ask your higher consciousness: Please show me what I am doing on my life-path when I suffer from feeling (emotion) about (problem).

- On our life-path, there are no problems—only challenges that we are happy to overcome. Therefore, when we suffer, it is a sign that we are straying from our life-path or standing still.

- After working with higher-consciousness healing for two weeks, you can ask this question again and see how the imagery has "improved."

Chapter 9

ASKING FOR A HEALING SYMBOL

NOW WE COME TO THE HEART OF higher-consciousness healing practice. After we have explored our problem with the life-path questions, we can ask for a healing symbol to overcome our suffering. It is important to use the exact same definition of our problem we formulated earlier (see chapter 4). Then ask your higher consciousness for a healing symbol in the following way:

Please give me a healing symbol to overcome my suffering from feeling (emotion) about (problem).

Someone who suffers from depression over not having a partner may ask: Please give me a healing symbol to overcome my suffering from feeling depressed about not having a partner. As I have explained before, that person should not ask: Please give me a symbol for finding a boyfriend. If we define a specific aim, as in the second example, we limit the possible ways in which our higher consciousness can solve our problem. But if we are completely open to whatever our higher consciousness wants to do to help us, the whole process is much more effective. As I was writing this, my friend Robert phoned me and told me about his latest results with higher-consciousness healing in solving his own financial worries. His story illustrates this dynamic quite clearly.

Robert

Robert retired early and worried a lot about money and about how to survive on his small pension as he got older. Sometimes, these worries were so bad that he felt panic-stricken. Two months before, he decided to use higher-consciousness healing to solve this problem. He measured his suffering from feeling anxious as 7 on the scale, and asked for a healing symbol. He received a beautiful gemstone, and after working with it for two weeks, he felt a lot calmer in himself. Then something astonishing happened. A chain of unlikely coincidences led him to the house of a friend of a friend in his favorite seaside town. They spent a lovely afternoon together and chatted about many things—among them, house prices. My friend learned, to his astonishment, that house prices in this seaside town were only half those in the town where he lived. In a flash, he realized that this could solve all his money problems. If he sold the house he lived in at the moment, he could not only move to his favorite seaside town, he would also have plenty of money for his old age. Robert has been 0 on the scale of money worries ever since.

• • •

This case study shows that higher-consciousness healing can bring solutions to our problems that are very unexpected and astonishing. Therefore, it is important to keep an open mind as to how our problem can be solved. If we are lucky, we may find that the solution is easier than we thought.

There is a multitude of possible healing symbols that may pop into our mind after we make our request to our higher consciousness. In order for a symbol to work, however, it needs to have a beautiful form and a bright color. A symbol that looks ugly or boring, or has a dark or dull color, cannot represent the solution to our problem. Here is a non-exhaustive list of possible healing symbols:

a brightly colored geometrical form

a piece of beautiful jewelry

gemstones

the sun or a shining star

a brightly colored animal

an angelic being surrounded by beautiful light

the blue sea or a green meadow

a brilliant white cloud in a radiantly blue sky

a brightly colored flower or a bunch of flowers

a bright green tree

How to Choose the Right Symbol

It is important that we only accept a healing symbol from our higher consciousness that we feel really good about. If we don't like our symbol, it won't be able to enter deeply into our unconscious mind and do the transformative work that is necessary. The following two examples illustrate this point.

A client of mine who suffered from depression received a beautiful red ruby as a healing symbol. When she came back to me, she complained that she hadn't improved one little bit. When I quizzed her about the details of her process, she told me that she had initially liked her red ruby, but then it reminded her of blood, which she found very repulsive. Obviously, she couldn't get better in that way. Her next symbol was a blue sapphire that helped her to overcome her depression beautifully.

Another client had a great problem with throwing anything away, so her apartment was filled with an incredible amount of stuff. She received a pink axe as a healing symbol, which seemed appropriate at first glance. I was suspicious, however, because usually the higher consciousness doesn't give such "aggressive" symbols. I asked my client how she felt about her healing symbol and, sure enough, she said she felt ambivalent about it. I suggested that she ask for a more pleasant symbol and, in the end, she received a pink heart, which she used successfully.

Don't take a symbol you feel ambivalent about.

If we receive a healing symbol that doesn't feel really good to us, for whatever reason, we should ask our higher consciousness for another.

Don't take a symbol you feel ambivalent about and don't try to change the symbol yourself. Always ask your higher consciousness to give you another symbol. One word of caution, however. If you haven't received a good healing symbol after three or four tries, give yourself a break and try again later. The part of your mind that can receive information on an intuitive level can tire quickly. This is especially true if you become impatient or frustrated.

Sometimes, people receive more than one symbol. If this happens, simply choose the symbol you like best.

The Importance of Bright Color

Different colors have different healing qualities. That is why they are used to cure emotional and physical problems in different forms of color therapy. Surprisingly, it doesn't seem to matter whether we experience "real" colored light from a lamp, or whether we just imagine it. The healing process works in either case. So when we work with higher-consciousness healing, we must always use a healing symbol with a bright and beautiful color. If our healing symbol is white, it needs to be a very radiant and brilliant white. In my experience, the following colors don't work for healing symbols:

black	brown
beige	gray
all dark colors	all pastel colors

If you receive a symbol that is one of these colors, or one that is transparent, simply ask your higher consciousness for a brighter color or for a new symbol altogether. For example, one acquaintance of mine had worked with higher-consciousness healing all by herself, but had achieved hardly any improvement with her anxiety disorder. When I asked her about her symbol, she said she had received a transparent ring. I told her that a transparent symbol doesn't work, and that her symbol needed to have a strong and radiant color. So she sat down and asked for another symbol. This time, she received a golden ring and her anxiety reduced greatly.

If you know a lot about color therapy, it is best if you put to one side your knowledge about which color traditionally cures which problem when you ask for your healing symbol. Instead, allow yourself to be surprised by the color your higher consciousness shows you. What matters is that you like your symbol. For example, in traditional color therapy, the color red is an invigorating color, while blue has calming properties. However, quite a few of my "anger clients" have successfully worked with bright-red symbols. Why that is I cannot say—I leave all this to the wisdom of the higher consciousness.

Trouble-Shooting

Once we have asked our higher consciousness for a healing symbol, it will just pop into our mind as anything ranging from a precise image to a vague thought. As I have said before, we don't have to visualize it clearly. If you have received only a vague idea about a symbol, just ask your higher consciousness if this is the right symbol for you, and check for an inner feeling of confirmation. If you get an inner feeling of "yes" (or at least not a "no"), and if you really like the symbol, go ahead and work with it. If you can't "see" your symbol at all, try making a simple drawing of it.

For most people, their symbol comes to them within a split second after asking their higher consciousness. So it is important to pay close attention so you don't miss it. Sometimes, people dismiss their first image and, afterward, feel as if their minds are blocked. To avoid this, try to acknowledge whatever comes into your mind. If you don't like what you see, you can simply ask for another symbol. We should never accept a symbol that has popped into our mind before we asked for it. We should always ask for our higher consciousness *first* and then see what pops into mind. If you still have problems receiving a symbol, here are some suggestions:

- Check to see if you have dismissed the first thought that came into your mind after asking for your healing symbol. If this is the case, ask your higher consciousness if your first thought was the right healing symbol.

- Maybe you expected to "see" a symbol, but instead "heard" an idea for a symbol. Maybe you even "felt" a symbol. Check to see if you received a symbol through a different channel from the one that you expected.

- Maybe you weren't relaxed enough to receive a symbol. Go back to your relaxation and try again a little later.

- Try to make your request for a symbol to your higher consciousness with more passion. Really mean it!

- Before you ask for your healing symbol, picture a lake. When you make your request to your higher consciousness, see a symbol emerging from the middle of the lake.

- Before you ask for your healing symbol, picture the dark night sky. When you make your request to your higher consciousness, see your symbol emerging out of the sky like a UFO.

- Before you ask for your healing symbol, picture a desert. When you make your request to your higher consciousness, see your symbol emerging like a mirage.

- Before you ask for a healing symbol, take a notepad and a pen. When you make your request to your higher consciousness, let your hand draw or write down an idea of a symbol.

- Before you ask for your healing symbol, imagine a radio. When you make your request to your higher consciousness, "hear" a response coming from this radio.

- Before you ask for your healing symbol, take a medium-sized piece of clay or something similar into your hands. When you make your request to your higher consciousness, let your hands form a rough symbol.

- If a friend or a therapist is guiding you through this part of higher-consciousness healing, they can ask your higher consciousness for a healing symbol on your behalf. They should ask out loud in the following way: *Please give (your name) a healing symbol to overcome his/her suffering from feeling (emotion) about (problem).* Listen to their request and then pay close attention to any idea of a symbol that may appear in your mind.

- If all else fails, let your friend or therapist receive a healing symbol on your behalf. Only accept a symbol that you really like.

Last, but not least, thank your higher consciousness once you are satisfied with the symbol of your choice.

John

John came to see me because he suffered from depression. Like many of my clients, he launched into a long explanation of why and how his depression had been caused by his alcoholic mother who had severely abused him when he was a child. After empathizing with John's feelings, I told him that—despite the popularity of these ideas—there is no proof that our current problems are caused by our childhood experiences. In actual fact, I have found that blaming our parents causes people to feel like victims and become even more depressed. To help John solve his problem, I showed him how to send love to himself and to his mother with the help of a healing symbol, and how to wish sincerely for himself and her to be happy. At the same time, I told him to relax the tensions in his chest that were associated with his depression. In that session, John completely dissolved all his depression, which hadn't happened in years. It took exactly four weeks before he could do this all by himself and feel joy and optimism in all areas of his life. Simultaneously, his relationship with his mother improved. To John's great surprise she started to phone him regularly, which was something she had never done before.

Summary

- Ask for your healing symbol in the following way: Please give me a healing symbol to overcome my suffering from feeling (emotion) about (problem).

- Your healing symbol must be beautiful and have a bright color.

- If you don't like your symbol, ask for another one.

- If you receive more than one symbol, pick the one that feels best for you.

Chapter 10

WORKING WITH OUR HEALING SYMBOL

IN THIS CHAPTER, WE'LL EXPLORE in more detail how to work with our healing symbol. Since a careful exploration may make the process appear more complicated than it is, I will first give you a short summary of how to do it.

1. See or sense your healing symbol in the middle of your chest.

2. While you breathe out, radiate the color of your healing symbol throughout your body and surround yourself with a bubble of loving joyful light.

3. When you breathe in, just relax. Then exhale the positive qualities of your symbol again.

4. If other people are involved in your problem, see them surrounded by bubbles of loving joyful light as well. Your bubble and theirs may touch, but they should not merge. Know that everyone who is genuinely happy will immediately repent their wrongdoing and become very likeable.

5. Relax the physical tensions that are associated with your painful emotions.

Quite a few of my "anxiety clients" immediately start to worry that they are not able to work with their healing symbols correctly. My advice is always the same: If it feels good, it will do you good. Working with your symbol should be an altogether pleasurable activity; at no time should it feel like a strain. Therefore, it is important not to worry about whether you are doing it correctly. If you get distracted, simply relax and come back to your healing symbol.

Our Spiritual Heart

In the middle of our chest, beneath our breastbone, is what I call our spiritual heart. It is from here that our deepest fulfillment and happiness arises. Our spiritual heart is the source of the love and the wisdom that we are all searching for and it is the only place where unhappiness can be transformed into happiness. Our spiritual heart is the place from which we can reconnect with our higher consciousness.

If we could experience our spiritual heart directly, we would experience only space—a space as wide as the universe and as bright as the sun, a space that is vibrant with the beautiful energy of love and joy. This space is the true nature of our being and the true nature of our higher consciousness. It is pregnant with possibilities. Anything can arise from it, including the solution to our problem. Into this space, we place our healing symbol. Don't think of your heart as a small physical organ, but as a limitless space that vibrates with love and joy. By putting our healing symbol into this space, we can connect more and more with our higher consciousness and gradually learn to receive the answers to all of our problems.

How does opening our heart contribute to finding happiness? Remember a time when you talked about a painful problem to someone and afterward you felt better. What exactly made you shift from unhappiness to happiness? Was it how you analyzed the problem when you talked about it? Was it the clarity of the advice you got from the other person? Probably not. When we are unhappy, our heart is closed. We feel better when our heart can open again, because this is the only way to reconnect to unconditional happiness. This opening of the heart is most likely to happen when someone listens to us in a sympathetic and appreciative way. The other person's sympathy comes directly from his or her heart and touches the hardened walls of ours. If we can surrender and allow ourselves to be touched in our most vulnerable spot, the walls and knots in our heart will melt away and we'll feel better again. Our emotional space can widen and fresh ideas about how to solve our problem may come to us.

Unfortunately, most of us don't have access to such a supportive listener all the time. However, higher-consciousness healing gives us the opportunity to get in touch with our spiritual heart and gently activate its power to transform unhappiness into happiness. When we visualize our healing symbol in the middle of our spiritual heart, the transformation of our problem comes from the most loving and sacred place within us. Doubts, confusion, and neurotic symptoms fade away and our self-confidence becomes much stronger. All our relationships improve, even if those involved in those relationships don't know about our practice. In other words, an open loving heart is part of the solution to all our problems.

Sometimes, people have difficulty visualizing their healing symbol clearly. It can appear vague and fragmented; it can disappear or become distorted; it can change into another symbol or even break apart. All this needn't be a problem. Simply return to your original symbol as it was given to you by your higher consciousness each time you lose it. If you have trouble visualizing, you can also make a simple drawing of your symbol and look at this picture instead of trying to visualize it.

Ruby I

The following case study stretches throughout the next two chapters, but it recounts just one single session with Ruby. The actual work with her symbol took roughly fifteen minutes. Ruby came to see me because she suffered from stress at work. In particular, she was afraid of a colleague who had been bullying her for a long time. On top of this, Ruby beat herself up for being unable to stand up to this colleague. Ruby was in a state of great anxiety while she was with me; she measured 8 out of 10 on the scale of fear (which is near to a panic attack). She received a blue flower as a healing symbol. After working with it for fifteen minutes, all her fear was dissolved and she was at 0 on the scale. For Ruby, who was in a chronic state of fear and self-loathing, that was a very unusual state. However, before we even started, Ruby had trouble visualizing her symbol and was very worried that she wouldn't do it correctly.

Therefore, I reassured her that the correct visualization wasn't necessary and asked her to draw a simple picture of her blue flower, which she did.

Radiating the Color of Our Symbol

The second step in this process is to let the color of our healing symbol radiate throughout our body and around ourselves with each out breath. The positive qualities of a symbol are transmitted through its color and its particular vibration. For example, the symbol of a bright yellow sunflower can stand for joy in life and childlike innocence. All these qualities are contained in its yellow color. So when we breathe out, we both feel and see how our body becomes filled with and surrounded by loving and joyful yellow light. As a result, our whole being becomes filled with the love and the meaning of our healing symbol. If we have a pink healing symbol, we lovingly breathe out pink light; if we have a blue symbol, we breathe out blue light. If we have received a healing symbol with two or more colors, we can choose one color on which to concentrate. Alternatively, we can visualize one color after the other; or we can visualize several colors together.

When practicing higher-consciousness healing, we must never force or exaggerate our breath. We should always inhale and exhale in a very relaxed and natural way. It is important always to breathe through our nose. After we have exhaled, we let the inhalation come in its own rhythm and simply relax. Then we breathe out again and let the healing light of your symbol radiate out once more.

> Never try to breathe in more deeply than you feel is natural.

In higher-consciousness healing, all the "activity" occurs on the out breath, never on the in breath. During inhalation, do nothing; simply relax. Only during the out breath do we visualize how the loving light of our symbol radiates out. There is an important reason for working in this way: Breathing out makes us relaxed; breathing in makes us tense. You can try this out. Simply breathe in deeply twenty times, filling your lungs to capacity. Most people will start to feel slightly tense and some will even develop a bit of headache or chest pain. By comparison, after concentrating on twenty relaxed out breaths, most people feel a lot calmer.

Unfortunately, some people have problems with all breathing exercises and they suddenly start to breathe in a strained and unnatural way. If this happens to you, please forget about the breathing part of the method. Just focus on your healing symbol and radiating its good qualities without connecting the process to your breath. If that works for you, it is better than creating new problems with the breathing part of the practice.

Antianxiety Breathing

The following breathing technique is a slight variation from what I have just explained and it can help with all problems that fall into the anxiety category—fear, panic, and nervousness. In order to calm all these emotions, we need to breathe *less*. When we are afraid, we breathe too fast and too much, and doing this changes our body chemistry, which strongly contributes to all forms of fear. When we can slow down our breathing, these painful feelings quickly die down. This is how it is done:

1. See your healing symbol in your heart and breathe out its color and good qualities with love as described before. It is most important always to breathe through your nose and never through your mouth.

2. Once you have breathed out, notice the gap before your next inhalation. Slowly, start to lengthen this gap by counting slowly as far as you get. Relax as much as you can while you count.

3. Breathe in again before you feel uncomfortable, and then immediately out again. (Never hold your in breath when you are scared, as this will strongly increase your anxiety!)

4. At the end of your out breath, count again as far as possible while relaxing more and more deeply. (Breathe in, breathe out, one . . . two . . . three . . . four . . . etc. . . . breathe in, breathe out, count . . . and so on.)

5. Carry on this breathing technique until your anxiety disappears. A relaxed person can have gaps of up to fifteen seconds between exhalation and inhalation.

This antianxiety breathing technique is very powerful and has brought profound relief to every single one of my clients suffering from fear, panic, or anxiety. To do it correctly, we do not need to achieve fifteen-second gaps between our out breaths and in breaths. But we do need to make sure that we never breathe through our mouth, that we never breathe in more deeply than feels comfortable, and that we never hold our breath.

Ruby II

I asked Ruby to look at her drawing of her symbol, to let its blue color radiate throughout her body, and to relax with every out breath. After doing this for one minute, Ruby relaxed a little bit and her fear went down from 8 to 7 on the scale. Then I showed her the antianxiety breathing technique. Like most chronically fearful people, Ruby had a habit of taking fast and shallow breaths through her mouth, which made her anxiety much worse. I instructed her to breathe through her nose and to count as far as possible at the end of each out breath. At first, Ruby could only count to three, but very quickly, her breathing slowed down and she could count to eight between each exhalation and inhalation. Simultaneously, her fear went down on the scale of suffering from 7 to 5.

Loving Ourselves

The core of all happiness is a feeling of love, and at the core of love are well-meaning wishes. For the transformation in higher-consciousness healing to occur, we do not have to be dependent on someone else to love us. We can simply love ourselves. At the same time, this love for ourselves can be part of the solution to our problem. No matter why we are suffering, more love is always part of the answer. Even if our problem is physical or financial, more love will help us to relax and be more content, despite external problems and adversity.

Loving ourselves is easy to talk about, but, for many of us, it is awkward to practice. For some, it even feels wrong, as if it will make them more self-indulgent, vain, or arrogant. Fortunately, this isn't true, because loving ourselves only makes us into a more loving and happy person who genuinely has something to give to others.

There is nothing strange about loving ourselves. People who have received an abundance of love throughout their childhood love themselves as the most natural thing in the world. They are often not even aware that they are doing it, because, for them, it's second nature. Those who have not received a lot of love throughout their lives, however, find it most difficult to love themselves. But they are the ones who need this love most urgently.

It is easy to love the parts of ourselves that are already perfect. If we want to solve our problems, however, we need to love ourselves in all our weakness and imperfection. Annie learned to love the parts of herself that she had hated before.

Annie

Annie was struggling with the problem of being overweight. When I told her that she should breathe the color and the good qualities of her healing symbol into her body with love, she looked at me with barely suppressed anger and said, "I don't love my fat—I hate it!" Luckily, she was also able to laugh about her anger. I explained to her that loving herself with all her imperfections didn't mean liking her fat. It simply meant sending the color and the positive qualities of her symbol to herself as a loving gift. What counted were her good intentions for her body, and that she stop hating herself and her fat. Annie understood what I meant and she breathed the color of her symbol into her body with the positive intention that her fat cells should transform in the most healthy and happy way. And it worked! Annie lost all the weight she wanted through some moderate changes in her diet and exercise program.

...

I have used higher-consciousness healing with a number of clients suffering from overweight, eating disorders, and alcohol addiction. They all, without exception, simply stopped overeating and drinking once they were able to send love to themselves with the help of a healing symbol.

Developing Love for Ourselves

Love is the core of higher-consciousness healing. It is, therefore, of paramount importance to get this part of the practice right. It is much more important than breathing properly or visualizing clearly. Here is a little exercise we can use to get a loving feeling going. We can use it each time we have trouble feeling the love from our healing symbol.

1. Think of someone whom you find easy to like and love. This may be your child, your partner, or even a pet. See this being in front of your inner eye and wish them to be happy with all your heart. Notice the warm feeling that arises in your chest when you make this wish.

2. Quickly, turn your loving intentions toward yourself without thinking or changing your feeling, and wish yourself to be happy from the bottom of your heart. Love yourself with all your weaknesses and imperfections like you would love a small unhappy child.

3. Visualize the love for yourself as a beautiful light that surrounds you like a bubble that is as big as your outstretched arms.

4. Alternatively, think of your higher consciousness sending love to you. Bathe in this bubble of love until you feel warm and happy.

5. Say very lovingly to yourself: I wish myself to be truly happy.

6. Each time you lose this warm feeling, go back to the beginning of this exercise and remember how it feels to be loving by thinking of someone you find easy to love. Then, quickly, turn this feeling of love to yourself and allow it to radiate throughout and around your whole being, together with the light of your healing symbol. Alternatively, think of your higher consciousness sending you love. Do whatever evokes a more loving feeling for yourself.

I once had a client who suffered from terrible anger and envy because she felt that everyone had a better life than she had. As with all my clients, when I showed her how to send love to herself, these extremely painful feelings subsided. This happened each time we worked in this way. Unfortunately, whenever this client was by herself, she tended to practice higher-consciousness healing in a mechanical way. Sadly, she was one of the very few clients who did not benefit from working with me. Therefore, it is paramount to generate a genuine feeling of love as I have described in the previous exercise. To my joy, 99 percent of the clients with whom I have worked in the last ten years could do this after a very short time and were able to reap the full benefits of this practice.

In higher-consciousness healing, we imagine that joyful love emerges from our healing symbol in our spiritual heart and radiates out to our entire body. Then the loving joyful light radiates beyond our body boundaries and surrounds us like a beautiful bubble. This bubble is roughly as big as our outstretched arms. Being in the bubble of joyful love feels wonderfully warm, secure, and happy. In addition, feeling the boundaries of our bubble gives our unconscious mind a strong message that we are totally safe and enables us to relate to others in a confident and loving way. If we feel anxious or if we are entangled in difficult relationships, we should reinforce this feeling of safety by repeatedly going around the firm boundaries of our bubble of love with our inner eye.

Ruby III

By now, Ruby had reduced her fear from 8 to 7 on the scale of suffering by filling her body with the blue light of her symbol, and then from 7 to 5 by using the antianxiety breathing technique. I then reminded her that the healing light from her symbol was full of love and asked her if she could feel this love. Unfortunately, Ruby could not. I asked her to visualize her small children in front of her inner eye and to wish them to be happy with all her heart by enveloping them with bubbles of loving joyful light. That was no problem for Ruby, and she felt a very warm feeling. I then asked her to surround herself with the same loving bubble of light and to say to herself "I wish myself to be truly happy," just as she had done with her children. Doing this was a sort of revelation for Ruby, who had suffered from self-loathing virtually all her life. To her delight, she discovered that it was perfectly within her reach to stop her self-loathing and to love herself instead. After bathing in the loving light for two minutes, her fear had reduced to 3 on the scale. I also asked her to go around the boundaries of her bubble with her inner eye and feel the sense of safety that this induced.

• • •

Sometimes, people start to feel sad when they concentrate on loving themselves. They may even end up in a state of heartbreaking self-pity. This, of course, should not happen. We must always remember that the light of our healing symbol is loving and joyful. People who have a tendency toward sadness should never forget to practice higher-consciousness healing with smiles on their faces.

Sending Love to Others

In the next step, we send the loving light of our healing symbol to everyone who is involved in our problem by surrounding them with bubbles of loving joyful light as well. Our bubbles may touch if we wish, but they should never overlap or merge.

Sending love to our adversaries is extremely liberating and will heal the effects of the most terrible traumas, as well as restore peace and harmony to our existing relationships. It is the very process of giving that makes us aware that there is an inexhaustible source of joy, love, and strength within us. Even better, through giving love, we genuinely dissolve all feelings of deprivation, helplessness, and victimization. Instead, we start to feel more confident, happy, and strong.

In my holistic life-coaching practice, I have worked with people who were abused sexually as children, who were raped or violently assaulted, and who were victims of domestic violence. I explain to all of them that it is not the actual trauma from the past that is causing their current problems, but their own current feelings of anger, resentment, or victimization. All these clients, without exception, experienced dramatic improvements in their overall well-being once they let go of these negative feelings by sending love to their assailants with the help of a healing symbol.

It is important to understand that sending love to someone who has harmed us does not mean that we forget what they did or take away their guilt. Nor does loving our adversaries mean liking the other person or simply to forgive. For example, if someone has abused a child, *no one* is in a position to forgive this terrible wrong; the aggressor has to live with the guilt for the rest of his or her life. Sending love to our enemies simply means to stop hating and resenting them and instead to wish them to be happy. Everyone who is happy will immediately regret all their wrongdoings and transform into a loving and really likeable person. Therefore, the most beneficial attitude we can have toward our adversaries is to send them love and good wishes. In other words, anger, resentment, and victim mentality tie us to traumatic events from our past; only love will set us free of them to embark on a life that is entirely free of the consequences of our terrible past traumas.

Sending love to others also works like a miracle in all sorts of difficult relationships. I have worked with quite a few couples on the brink of divorce, with people with strained family relations, and with clients with all sorts of other relationship problems. All of them either dramatically improved their relationships by working out their conflicts, or finally became able to withdraw from abusive individuals. It is important to understand that loving our enemies doesn't mean that we stay close to a cruel person or just put up with someone's wrongdoing without asserting our needs. It is crucial that we learn to keep a clear distance from abusive people and to continue a relationship only once we have received a credible apology and amends. The image of the firm bubbles that surround us and everyone who is involved in our problem will help us to stabilize our ego boundaries so that we can do just that.

Sending love to someone who has harmed us may seem to go against all our natural instincts. But all wise people say that "loving our enemies" is the solution to all our problems. By comparison, punching pillows and shouting angrily—as is, regrettably, done in several forms of therapy—will only aggravate our anger. You can try this out. For ten minutes, hit a pillow with all your might and shout angrily at everyone who has ever hurt you. You will find that you become physically exhausted, and you might also experience a short-lived sense of liberation. But then you will find that, on a mental level, your anger quickly returns—and often stronger than before. The only genuine, lasting, and complete solution that overcomes the effects of past traumas and problems in relationships is love.

It is important to include our parents in our loving wishes—especially if we feel resentment toward them. In my counseling practice, I have observed that it is outright impossible to become happy and successful if we still resent our parents. This is true even if our parents have behaved in an abusive or neglectful way. The reason for this is that when we hate our parents, we actually hate ourselves. I like to explain this dynamic with the image of a flowerbed. We are the flower and our parents are the flowerbed from which we grow. By resenting our flowerbed, we poison it. As a result, we can't grow into our full potential. But when we wish our parents to be happy (no matter how much wrong they have done in our upbringing), we help create a nourishing and fertile flowerbed from which we can grow into the most beautiful and lush plant.

In order to send love to our adversaries, we need to imagine them, one by one, in front of our inner eye (as far away or as near as feels comfortable). Then we imagine that the loving light from our healing symbol envelopes them within a bubble of love. In our mind, we say to this person: I wish you to be happy. If we feel regret or guilt toward them, we can say: I am sorry for what I have done and I wish you to be happy. Or I am sorry it didn't work out and I wish you to be happy. However, sending love to others doesn't just mean always speaking in a sugary voice. Quite the contrary. In my life-coaching practice, I have seen that this actually enables fearful people to stand up for their rights and speak with firm clarity. Ruby's story shows this quite clearly.

Ruby IV

After Ruby had enveloped herself in a bubble of loving joyful light, I asked her to send love to her bullying colleague and to see him within a bubble of loving joyful light as well. At first, she was very reluctant. "I want to hate and punish him," she said with emphasis. I explained to her that it was in her own interest that her colleague be happy, because he would then stop bullying her. Finally, Ruby agreed. She sent the healing light of her symbol to her colleague and imagined that it would make him into someone happy and easy to get along with. As a result, her fear decreased even further—from 3 to 2 on the scale of suffering. Also, a lot of resentment she had felt along with her fear simply vanished. For the first time since working with her colleague, Ruby caught an intuitive glimpse into his psyche and realized just how unhappy he was in himself. This insight evoked some compassion in her and she felt much more confident than before. I then encouraged her to send the light of her healing symbol to her father, whom she resented for being too strict with her when she was a child.

. . .

It is important never to let our bubbles of loving joyful light merge or overlap, as this may result in unhealthy submission and dominance. There is only one exception to this rule: Our own children, before the age of puberty, can be visualized within our own bubble of light. In all other cases, the bubbles may touch if we feel very fond of the other person, or they may be very far away from each other if we want to maintain distance from our adversary. For example, we can visualize a difficult person two miles away so that he or she appears as a tiny speck on the horizon.

Sometimes, our bubbles of joyful love may seem to take on a life of their own and do things that they are not supposed to do. For example, they may distort, they may become very small, they may break, or they may start to merge. It may also appear that we or the other person do not want to stay within these bubbles. In all these cases, we should mentally interrupt this and simply return to our healthy image of two arms-length-sized bubbles of joyful love that may touch, but do not overlap. If we have continuing problems with people "escaping" from their bubbles, we can even imagine that everyone is fastened with a seat belt within their bubbles of love. We can also visualize a glass wall between the two bubbles that will keep them separate. With time and practice, our inner image will remain more stable.

Relaxing Emotional Tensions in Our Body

Many people find that their negative emotions subside a good deal when they send love to themselves and others with the help of their healing symbols. However, the final letting go of negative emotions usually happens through relaxing the physical tensions that go along with them. Every single negative feeling manifests in our physical body as tension. Once we have identified where these tensions are (see chapter 3) we simply and patiently have to relax them with every out breath. In that way, we can free ourselves from a lifetime of crippling emotions within a few weeks. By learning to relax the tensions of our negative emotions, we naturally arrive at the unconditional happiness that is the natural state of our being and that was there all along.

Therefore, after we have sent love to ourselves and others, we allow the light of our healing symbol to radiate into the part of our body that holds the tensions of our negative emotions. With every out breath, we relax these tensions just as if we were opening up a tight fist. We can help this process along by imagining that our emotional pain is like a tight flower bud that opens up into a beautiful flower with each exhalation.

Sometimes, we have to focus on relaxing our negative emotions over and over, because our habitual tensions may quickly return if we don't pay attention. It is important not to become discouraged by this dynamic. If we patiently relax all the physical tensions of our negative emotions, we will find that our painful feelings come back less frequently and with less strength. And eventually, they will stay away completely. In effect, doing this work is a way of retraining our body and mind to stay relaxed and happy. To my joy, virtually all my clients were able to decrease their negative emotions significantly and, if they kept at it, to dissolve them completely after a few days or weeks by using this approach.

In order to achieve these dramatic results, we need to become aware of even the tiniest amount of emotional tension and to relax immediately, before it can build up to a full-blown emotion. For example, one of my clients called her feelings of depression "her tsunami," which implied that her depression came in waves. I told her that as soon as she felt "a tsunami" rolling in, she should relax her eyes and the top of her head, where she usually felt these negative feelings. After practicing in this way for two weeks, she was virtually symptom-free.

Sometimes, people feel their negative emotions in several parts of the body. For example, people may feel irritation in the stomach, jaw, and arms. As usual, we always start with the most painful emotion. Once we have relaxed that part of our body, we move to the next strongest emotion and dissolve all tensions, one after the other.

Ruby V

So far, Ruby had reduced her anxiety from 8 to 2 by slowing down her breathing and sending love to herself and her bullying colleague. I then asked her where in her body she felt the remaining anxiety; she said in her stomach. I instructed her to send the loving light of her healing symbol to her solar plexus and to see it opening up like a beautiful flower. It took about two minutes for her anxiety to disappear completely. This was a major breakthrough, because Ruby had been chronically anxious for years and had rarely experienced moments of inner peace—let alone at a time of conflict with a bullying colleague. I instructed her to carry on at home, to slow down her breathing, and to send love to herself, her colleague, and her father.

When Ruby returned to me two weeks later, she told me that she had sent love to her colleague and her father on a daily basis. To her joy, she felt a lot more confident and at peace with her father. To her even greater amazement, her colleague had become much friendlier toward her. Simultaneously, her anxiety decreased to almost 0. Interestingly, she suddenly had the courage to complain to her superiors and demand that this man be removed from her department. Her manager had long known that Ruby's colleague was a troublemaker, and her complaint was the last piece of evidence needed to take disciplinary action against him. Over the next few months, Ruby's situation at work improved dramatically, along with her self-esteem.

· · ·

When we use higher-consciousness healing to remove pain from our body we work exactly in the same way. We assume that our pain is just a form of tension and we relax this tension as we allow the color of our healing symbol to penetrate the part of our body that feels painful.

Relaxing physical tension can also be used to dissolve chronic tiredness (the kind of tiredness that does not come from a lack of sleep). Most people think that they need more energy when they feel tired. This belief is incorrect, however. Chronic tiredness is a state of tension that suppresses our energy. Therefore, instead of trying to "build up" more energy, we simply need to relax the tensions that go along with our fatigue.

Ramona

Ramona had been diagnosed with chronic fatigue twenty years ago, and had been treated with numerous naturopathic remedies without much success. After she received her healing symbol, I showed her how to look for the tensions that produced the feeling of fatigue. At first, she was reluctant and insisted that her tiredness was "everywhere." Once I guided her through her body, however, she could identify her tiredness as tension in her temples. Then I showed her how to relax these tensions with every out breath with the help of her healing symbol. In her mind's eye, she saw these tensions opening out like beautiful flowers over and over. Ramona's fatigue was particularly bad that day, but after five minutes of practicing higher-consciousness healing, it was virtually gone. To her surprise, she suddenly felt "quite normal."

Overcoming Depression with a Smile

Smiling is beneficial for reducing all sorts of negative emotions, but it is particularly important for all emotions from the sadness category—depression, feeling low, or emotional hurt. By smiling, we help to jumpstart a positive feeling that will replace our sadness and depression.

It couldn't be easier. We just focus on the joyful quality of the light radiating from our healing symbol by putting a smile on our face. Then we allow this positive feeling to radiate through our being. We do not hang on to our sadness by wondering where it has gone, or whether it had something important to tell us. Instead, we remember that our true being is always happy and joyful, and that smiling simply reminds us of that fact. Simultaneously, we identify the physical tensions that go along with our feeling of depression and patiently relax these tensions with every out breath, as described above. Most people feel depressive feelings in their head, eyes, or chest area.

Working with our symbol and smiling also stops the negative self-talk that most people who suffer from depression repeat to themselves. Instead of telling ourselves that everything is hopeless and that we are doomed to fail, we put our mind on our symbol and a smile on our face. In that way, we can determinedly cut though any of our negative thoughts. It is not necessary to replace our negative thoughts with positive thoughts, because this can be very difficult and exhausting. We just keep our mind on our loving healing symbol and focus on a relaxed and joyful smile, and our depressive thoughts will have nowhere to manifest themselves. We may then find to our surprise that positive thoughts spontaneously enter our mind.

Harriet

Harriet suffered from lifelong depression that had no particular cause and seemed to be "free floating." She also had many depressive thoughts: "I am failure" (she was successful in her career and had many friends) and "Nothing will ever change for the better" (she had overcome a serious illness and her relationship with her parents had vastly improved during the last ten years). Harriet realized that her negative thoughts were irrational, but because they popped into her head frequently, she thought they were somehow true. I told her that she had to get firm with her negative thoughts and that the light of her symbol was like a knife that could cut through these thoughts before they darkened her emotional landscape. I also showed her how to smile in order to jump-start a positive feeling and how to release the tensions in her chest that went along with her depression. Harriet practiced in this way and was able to reduce her depression dramatically within four weeks. As a result, she started to go to a drama group and joined a spiritual circle. This further improved her well-being, and her lifelong depression was soon a thing of the past.

Bringing It All Together

When we first work with a healing symbol, it is useful to spend some time on each part of the practice—visualizing the symbol, breathing correctly, creating bubbles of loving light for ourselves and others, relaxing emotional tensions, and smiling. But it will quickly become apparent which of these parts brings us the most relief. Then we can spend the most time on this aspect of the method. For example, some people find that sending love to themselves brings the most relief; others find that relaxing their negative emotion is the most liberating.

We can use our own inner guidance to decide on which part of the practice we want to focus most strongly. We can simply go with what feels best. Just make sure that love is part of your approach, because this is the core of higher-consciousness healing. With time, simply remembering your symbol will spontaneously evoke in you love, relaxation, and a joyful feeling.

Summary

- See or sense your healing symbol in your spiritual heart in the middle of your chest.

- While you breathe out, radiate the color of your healing symbol throughout your body and see yourself surrounded by a bubble of love. Love yourself, including all your weaknesses, by wishing yourself to be happy.

- When you breathe in, just relax. Then exhale the positive qualities of the symbol again.

- If other people are involved in your problem, envelope them within a bubble of loving joyful light as well. Wish the other person happiness and know that everyone who is happy immediately repents their wrongdoings and becomes very likeable.

- If you harbor resentment toward your parents, always send love to them as well.

- If you still feel negative emotions, relax the tensions that are associated with them.

- If you feel anxious, combine higher-consciousness healing with the antianxiety breathing technique.

- If you feel sad or depressed, put a smile on your face while you practice.

PRACTICING THE METHOD

Chapter 11

FORMAL AND INFORMAL PRACTICE

AFTER WE HAVE RECEIVED our healing symbol in relaxation, we work with it as described in the previous chapter in a formal practice for a minimum of two minutes, twice a day. We should also practice it informally every time our negative feelings come up. In order to achieve lasting results with higher-consciousness healing, we have to work with our healing symbol for at least two weeks.

Creating a Regular Formal Practice

For our formal practice, it is best to find a time when we have enough peace and quiet to concentrate fully on our healing symbol. Most people agree that it is always possible to squeeze four minutes into their daily routines, no matter how tight their schedules. The easiest way to create a new habit is to add it on to a habit that already exists. For example, we can practice immediately after getting up or right after we have cleaned our teeth. One of my clients always focuses on his symbol on the train to and from work. For most people, just trying to remember to practice their symbols does not work.

In order to achieve lasting results with higher-consciousness healing, we need to work with our healing symbol twice a day for two weeks—twenty-eight times in all. If we forget to do the practice for a day or two, we can simply add those sessions on at the end of our two weeks. For example, if, on average, we forget half of our sessions, we work with our symbol for four weeks instead of two. All that matters is that we do not give up altogether.

Sometimes, people work with a symbol for a few days, and as soon as their problems improve, they stop. This is not advisable, because often the problem will return quickly. It is important always to complete at least a two-week period with each symbol. If our problem has not completely resolved itself within two weeks, we can carry on with the same symbol as long as we feel is necessary.

Using Our Symbol Informally

In addition to our formal practice, it is important to use our symbol every time our negative self-talk and painful feelings associated with our problem come up. This sounds more difficult than it is. We do not need to interrupt our activities or close our eyes in order to practice in daily life. It is enough if our symbol flickers through our mind every now and then, and if we can think vaguely of the bubbles of loving light surrounding ourselves and others. We can do this while having a conversation, while reading a book, or while working.

Many of my clients have commented on how easy and helpful it is to focus on their symbols in difficult situations instead of being overwhelmed by their negative thoughts and emotions. For example, one of my clients suffered from social phobia. Every time she had to confront a crowd of people, she concentrated on her symbol and slowed down her breathing. Doing this took her mind right off her anxiety and cut through her old negative habit. Within four weeks, her phobia almost disappeared, and she has needed to go back to her symbol only very rarely. Her example is typical.

The earlier we notice our negative feelings, the better, because it is a lot easier to cut through small emotions than through fully grown temper tantrums. There is no danger in suppressing our emotions with higher-consciousness healing. Instead, we genuinely transform and heal them by replacing them with the loving and healing light of our symbol. In that way, our problem is positively resolved.

Sometimes, people feel swamped by negative emotions and feel that they have to focus on their symbols all the time. Luckily for most people, these trying times quickly get better with a good night's sleep. During sleep, our symbol can move even more deeply into our unconscious mind and set things right at the root. In that way, virtually everyone finds that negative emotions lessen—abruptly or gradually—and eventually disappear altogether.

Stopping Negative Self-Talk

It is very important to notice any form of negative self-talk and to cut through it before it can develop into a painful emotion. We can do this by placing our mind on our healing symbol. In order to distinguish negative self-talk from healthy and constructive self-criticism, we can ask ourselves: Would I talk in this critical way to my most beloved friend? If the answer is no, then we shouldn't talk to ourselves in this negative way either. As a general rule, most depressed people suffer from negative self-talk, as do most anxious people. They all benefit from dropping this negative habit and sending love to themselves instead with the help of their healing symbols.

We don't have to try hard to think positively. Trying hard to think positively can quickly develop into a form of inner battle, in which our positive and negative voices fight with each other. All we have to do in higher-consciousness healing is replace our negative thought with a positive image of our healing symbol radiating with love. When we do this, positive thoughts often arise spontaneously.

We don't have to try hard to think positively.

Obviously, these positive thoughts are there for us to retain and enjoy.

The more quickly we stop our negative thoughts, the more quickly we will be successful. For example, don't think: Oh, my legs are so ugly. Instead, stop yourself before this nasty thought has finished and quickly put your mind on your healing symbol. This will keep the negative thought from developing into a painful emotion. This is not hard to do, but I admit that, sometimes, it can be a bit tedious—like cleaning up our kitchen day in and day out. But the good news is that our "inner cleaning activities" will become less frequent the more we focus on our healing symbol instead of sliding back into our old emotional habits. It is certainly possible to retrain our mind, and after only a few days or weeks, our negative inner voices will give up.

We cannot really overdo higher-consciousness healing. Even if we focus on our healing symbol all day long, it can only be beneficial and we will never get any negative side effects.

Ruby VI

Ruby (whom you met in the previous chapter) had a persistent habit of negative self-talk. She was born and raised in a country that sees women as subordinate, and she had lived through an arranged marriage with a violent man. Every day, she called herself things like "stupid cow" and blamed herself for every little thing that went wrong around her, even if it had nothing to do with her. When I told Ruby that this negative self-talk was the first thing she had to stop, she was surprised and confused. It never had occurred to her that she was harming herself by talking to herself in that negative way. However, she made a strong effort to cut through this very bad habit by placing her mind on her healing symbol each time a self-reproach came up. She quickly became better at it. After only two months, she completely stopped calling herself names and, instead, was able to send a strong feeling of love to herself. At first, she felt slightly sad that she had made her life such a misery with her negative self-talk, but this sadness quickly disappeared. To Ruby's surprise, she suddenly had much more energy and she used this new-found energy to train for a marathon. She also joined a spiritual community where she hoped to find a new partner—this time, one she chose herself.

Don't Change Your Symbol

In some of the rare cases when clients have reported that their symbols haven't worked, it turned out that they had allowed their healing symbols to change or that they had changed them themselves. This was the case for Mary.

Mary

Mary had been working on her problem of depression quite successfully. When we first met, she had arrived at 7 on the scale of suffering. After four weeks of higher-consciousness healing, her suffering was down to 1. However, when she came to her next session, she felt dreadful again. When I asked her what had happened, she told me that she felt that her healing symbol had gradually "lost its power." She didn't feel excited by it anymore, and she found it harder and harder to visualize in its original form (a happy person standing on top of a mountain). The symbol seemed to be changing and looked more like a lonely woman in the rain. Mary had just been going along with this change and visualizing the symbol in its new and negative form. Not surprisingly, she felt worse and worse. I explained that practicing her new and more negative symbol was increasing her inner negativity. Luckily, after realizing her error, Mary returned to her original symbol and soon felt better again.

. . .

Never allow your healing symbol to change and never change it yourself. Every time your healing symbol seems to change its form or color, immediately return to your original symbol, as it was given to you by your higher consciousness. It doesn't matter how often you have to repeat this process, because it will not weaken the positive effects of higher-consciousness healing.

Work Actively to Solve the Problem

When we use our symbol, we must work actively toward the solution of our problem and do everything that common sense dictates. Don't just sit back and do nothing, while hoping that your higher consciousness will solve all your problems. Unfortunately, it just doesn't work that way. The following parable exemplifies this point:

Nasreddin and the Flood

A big flood had engulfed the country and Nasreddin sat on top of a tree well above the water. Nasreddin was a very religious man. He fervently prayed to God to save him and he felt total faith in his heart that this would happen. When a boat appeared and the people in it offered to rescue Nasreddin, he declined and told them that he was sure God would save him. The people in the boat tried to convince him to join them, but finally they gave up and went away. Another boat appeared, but Nasreddin declined again. The water rose and rose and, finally,

Nasreddin had to let go of the tree and swim in the water. Again he prayed to God to save him and again he felt optimistic that this would happen. A helicopter appeared, but Nasreddin once again declined to be rescued. As before, he told the people that God would save him. Nasreddin swam for three days and three nights in the water. Then his strength failed and he drowned.

When Nasreddin appeared in heaven in front of God's throne, he was furious. "I prayed to you to save me," he said angrily, "but you let me drown! Didn't you hear my prayers?"

"I heard your first prayer," God said in a mild way, "and I sent you a boat. But you declined its help. Then I heard your second prayer and I sent another boat, but you declined that help as well. I also heard your third prayer and, that time, I sent you a helicopter. But again, you declined its help. What else, Nasreddin, could I have done for you?"

. . .

This story encourages us to use common sense and take every bit of help that is offered to us. Sometimes, higher-consciousness healing will support us in doing the most obvious thing—the one that was always in front of our nose. At other times, we may even be lucky enough to experience a small miracle. Therefore, always be active and try to improve your situation in whatever way you can.

For those who find it difficult to get up and do something about their problems, here is another piece of good news. I have observed that people who previously just put up with their problems passively suddenly become active in finding solutions when they start practicing higher-consciousness healing. Their healing symbol seems to remove the block that hindered them from being disciplined and active in solving their problems.

Attracting Other Forms of Help

Higher-consciousness healing is not an exclusive method. It can work as a catalyst to trigger other processes that can help us solve our problems. For example, sometimes we "coincidentally" find a book that gives us much-needed insights; sometimes, we "coincidentally" meet a person who can help us. The following case study demonstrates this dynamic in quite a dramatic way.

Brenda

Brenda suffered from a very painful spinal disorder that was so disabling that she couldn't go to work; she lived on benefits. When she talked to me, she felt so depressed that she was suicidal. I immediately helped her to receive a symbol to dissolve her despair. When I heard from her two months later, she told me an astounding and unlikely story. Brenda had long been convinced that she would get optimal treatment in a special hospital in another country, but she had never had the financial means to get there. After starting to work with her symbol, Brenda's depression lifted and she wrote to an airline to ask for a free ticket, which she promptly received. She flew to the other country, simply turned up at the hospital, and asked for treatment. To her joy, she received treatment worth many thousands of dollars and was allowed to pay it back in very small installments. She even received free lodging. Her condition dramatically improved and she returned home with new hope. Brenda put all these unlikely coincidences down to her practice of higher-consciousness healing. Obviously, I cannot say if this is so. What I can say is that I have seen "miracles"—some small and some large—when people start to connect with their higher consciousness and send love to their problems.

Overcoming Emotional Problems

Some people believe that in order to overcome their problems, all they need is one amazing breakthrough in which everything becomes clear and their problem is solved once and for all. In my experience, it doesn't work like this. The human mind seems to need time and frequent reminders to make lasting changes.

Many problems are nothing other than habits of negative thinking and negative feeling. In order to overcome them, we have to let them go and replace them with positive rational beliefs and more joyful feelings. This may sound terribly simplistic, but when it comes to changing the human mind, it boils down to just that. Even if we have deep insights and amazing liberating experiences, the resulting positive emotions will often be short-lived if we don't know how to engrain these changes into our mind. Repeating our healing symbol twice a day over the course of two weeks helps us achieve this.

Some people try to change their negative habits of thinking and feeling with just their willpower. This usually doesn't work, because it doesn't take into account the part of us that wants, unconsciously, to hold on to our problem. My client Paul is a good example of this.

Paul

Paul had problems with commitment in his relationships with women and had just left his wife. He moved in with his girlfriend, but they were arguing a lot because she wanted more commitment than he was willing to give. Paul had spent much of his adult life under the influence of drugs and alcohol, and had only made a half-hearted commitment to stop this. He was pretty depressed about his whole situation, but he was motivated to bring about some change. His favorite approach was to use affirmations, like "I am fully alive and happy" or "I now commit joyfully." He used to say positive statements to himself, and if he felt he was resisting them, he simply repeated them to himself more often. Unfortunately, the use of positive affirmations did not help him. On the contrary, they usually made him feel worse. The more he tried to talk himself into these affirmations, the more the impulse not to commit surfaced and the more a voice in his head told him that his life was meaningless. But Paul was undeterred and struggled on, repeating his sentences in the hope that, one day, he would break through his own resistance.

Once Paul began to use symbols, his situation improved. After several days of sending love to his wife and to his girlfriend, he did what he had avoided doing all his life and what he feared most of all. He talked openly to his wife and to his girlfriend, and started to relate to them in a more honest way. This was a major breakthrough for Paul, because throughout his adult life, he had never related to anyone in an honest way. His relationships were always riddled with lies and dishonesty. For him to have the courage to talk to someone honestly was a mini-enlightenment. His depression lifted considerably, and by the time he stopped coming to see me, he was about to move out of his girlfriend's flat. It had become clear to him that he was at a stage in his life where he didn't want to make a commitment, and that it was in the best interest of everyone that he live on his own for a while.

...

Some people believe that it is possible to "let feelings out" by screaming and hitting pillows. Unfortunately, the opposite is true. People who express their negative emotions frequently and powerfully soon discover that their emotions increase and become more difficult to control. The whole idea that we can somehow expel negative emotions from our body is completely wrong. Emotions are not "things" that can be moved from one place to another. They are mental experiences that can easily become destructive habits. The sublime pacifier of all negative emotions is love for ourselves and for others. Higher-consciousness healing enables us to heal our negative emotions with love without suppressing them.

Another destructive attitude that keeps people from finding happiness is blaming others. Unfortunately, in our society, it is still widely believed that childhood experiences or other traumas from the past are somehow to blame for present problems. I always explain to my clients that there is no proof of these theories, even if millions of people believe in them. One thing is absolutely certain, however—blaming others leads to a victim mentality, chronic resentment, and depression. Higher-consciousness healing offers a radical and extremely quick way to overcome all real and imagined consequences of past traumas—sending love to the very people who have hurt us. In that way, our victim mentality is replaced with confidence, resentment is replaced with inner peace, and depression can easily be transformed into *joie de vivre*. Karen's story illustrates this point quite clearly.

Karen

Karen contacted me because nothing in her life was as she wished it to be. She had no boyfriend; she didn't like her work; she thought it was impossible to get a visa for the country she wanted to live in. Karen was consumed by envy and was convinced that "everybody had what they wanted" and that "she was irreparably scarred by her upbringing." She freely admitted that her parents had been quite loving, however, but she was adamant that something in her childhood must be to blame for all her problems. After searching high and low, she finally concluded that it had to be the fact that she was an only child. She had subscribed to a website that encouraged her in this belief and was full of self-pity when she contacted me. She was quite taken aback when I (gently) disagreed with her conviction. Fortunately, after working first on her chronic resentment with one symbol and on her envy with another, she felt so much better that she confessed to me that "all this whining" of the people on her website about the effects of being an only child was really getting on her nerves. Several months later, she contacted me with the positive news that she felt strongly inspired to become a counselor herself and—even better—that this would allow her to get a student visa so she could live and study in the country of her dreams. She had changed from being a resentful, envious, and depressed person to one who was responsible, positive, and in control.

Summary

- Work with your healing symbol for two minutes, twice a day, for two weeks in formal practice.

- Use your symbol every time negative feelings around your problem arise.

- Determinedly stop all negative self-talk by placing your mind on your healing symbol as soon as a negative thought arises.

- Never allow your healing symbol to change of its own accord and never change it yourself.

- Actively work for the solution of your problem as common sense dictates.

- Avoid misconceptions about how to solve emotional problems, like using too much willpower, forcefully expressing negative emotions, or blaming others.

Chapter 12

GETTING FEEDBACK ON OUR PROCESS

AFTER FINISHING TWO WEEKS of higher-consciousness healing, most people experience a significant improvement in their suffering. There are two ways in which we can get feedback on our progress.

Consulting the Scale of Suffering

To get feedback on your progress with higher-consciousness healing, ask yourself where you are on the scale of suffering (taking an average of the last three days), and then compare this number with the one from two weeks before. In order to get a correct reading, it is important to go back to the precise definition of your problem and to measure only the negative emotion that you have been addressing. For example, if you defined your problem as "suffering from feeling afraid of arguments with my partner" and measured your fear as 8 on the scale, now look at how much your fear has decreased and not at how many arguments you have had, or if you feel any other negative emotions, like anger, for example.

In many cases, people experience quite dramatic improvements. They may initially measure their suffering the first time as 7 or 8; after two weeks, they may be down to 2 or 3. Even if you don't get this major improvement, however, it is good to appreciate any improvement you have achieved. This will increase your confidence and determination to carry on.

In rare cases, our initial negative emotion may be replaced with a different one. For example, we may find that we are no longer afraid, but that we feel quite annoyed instead. This may seem frustrating, but it is actually a positive development. It simply means that we have worked through the first layer of our emotions and can now work (with a different symbol) on the next layer. There are only three layers (anxiety, sadness, and anger), and most people experience only one sort of negative emotion per problem. In the next chapter, I will say more about how to work through complex problems.

It is a good idea to write down all our scale numbers so we don't miss any positive improvements.

Consulting Our Life-Path

The second way to get feedback on our process is to ask our higher consciousness to show us our progress on our life-path. This is a more intuitive approach compared with consulting the scale of suffering, and as I have said before, it is not essential for higher-consciousness healing to work. So if the imagery of the life-path doesn't appeal to you, you can leave it out altogether.

Before you can consult your life-path, recall where you were on your life-path and what you were doing two weeks ago. If you have made progress with your problem, your higher consciousness should show you that you are moving forward with more confidence—for example, walking upward instead of standing still. You may even find that you are a bit farther up on your life-path. In order to consult your life-path, just relax. Then you can ask your higher consciousness in the following way:

Please, can you show me what I am doing now on my life-path?

As before, watch out for the very first thought or image that pops up in your head. For most people, the imagery of the life-path is quite self-explanatory. Here is a list of what may indicate a positive improvement. For more explanations about the life-path, please return to chapter 8.

- Your life-path is more visible than before.

- You have turned toward your higher consciousness.

- You are now on your life-path instead of next to it or on other paths.

- You are standing up instead of sitting down.

- You are moving in the right direction.

- You have increased your speed.

- The obstacles on your path (rocks, streams, etc.) have become smaller, have disappeared, or you have found a way around them.

- The weather is better.

Here are some examples of how my clients' life-path imagery has changed in the process of practicing higher-consciousness healing.

Table 3. Life-Path Imagery Changes

Life-path imagery at the beginning	Life-path imagery after two weeks	Life-path imagery after using four weeks
Halfway up the mountain	A few meters higher up	Even higher up
Sitting and looking downward into the valley	Still sitting, but looking up to the higher consciousness	Starting to walk to the higher consciousness
A big rock obstructs the life-path	The rock has disintegrated into smaller rocks	The path is clear

Appreciating Our Improvement

Getting feedback on our process is important for two reasons. First, it serves as an encouragement and helps us to keep going. Second—and this is even more crucial—it gives us an opportunity to appreciate our effort. This is extremely important, because each time we consciously appreciate our ability to solve our problems, we become more confident, more able, and more in control. In that way, we benefit doubly from higher-consciousness healing—we get rid of our problem *and* we gain the confidence to solve all our future challenges as well.

Unfortunately, I have seen people who achieved dramatic results with higher-consciousness healing, but because they were not able to appreciate these improvements, never experienced an overall confidence boost. Even more sadly, these people quickly forgot about this method and felt as helpless as before.

Gary

Gary suffered from exhaustion and chronic fatigue. When he asked for his life-path imagery, he saw himself lying on his life-path sleeping. I asked him where in his body he felt his tiredness, and after much searching, he realized that he felt tension in his head. After he received his healing symbol, I showed him how to release and relax that tension with every out breath by imagining a beautiful flower opening up in his head.

Unfortunately, Gary's progress was slow, because he always thought that the reasons for his tiredness came from outside his mind (hard work, a virus, etc.), and that he would be unable to do something about it himself. Not surprisingly, after two weeks, he saw himself still lying on his life-path—but at least his eyes were half open. This coincided with feeling a little bit less tired (from 7 to 5 on the scale). I explained to Gary that his higher consciousness has so much energy that it can light up half of the universe for a week. The solution to his fatigue was to let the light of his higher consciousness release the energy in his body that had been there all along.

Gary accepted my line of thinking and concentrated strongly to intercept even the tiniest amount of tiredness before it crept in by immediately relaxing the tension in his head. Slowly, his condition improved and so did the imagery on his life-path. After two months, he was finally standing up; after three months, he was energetically walking up the mountain. His chronic tiredness completely disappeared, despite his working even harder than before.

Summary

- After two weeks, measure your amount of negative emotion on the scale (take an average of the last three days) and compare the number with the one you had two weeks earlier.

- Ask your higher consciousness for your current life-path imagery and compare it with the one you received two weeks earlier. Ask in the following way: *Higher consciousness, can you please show me what I am doing now on my life-path?*

- Your life-path imagery will improve according to how you have improved with your problem.

- Try to appreciate sincerely even the smallest improvements.

Chapter 13

WORKING WITH COMPLEX PROBLEMS

IF YOU WANT TO ADDRESS A COMPLEX problem and you know in advance that it has several aspects and layers (like the suffering arising from a divorce), always work first with the negative emotion that causes you the most suffering. For example, ask yourself whether you feel mostly anger, mostly sadness, or mostly fear. As I have pointed out before, it is important to avoid psychoanalyzing yourself to find "deeper aspects" or "unconscious motivations." It is much more important to pinpoint your most painful emotion clearly and then to dissolve it by using a healing symbol.

Once your initial negative emotion has been substantially reduced (after two to four weeks), you may find that another negative emotion comes to the foreground. This is a very good sign of progress. Simply ask for another healing symbol to overcome this new aspect of your problem. There are only three main categories of negative emotions: anger, sadness, and anxiety (see chapter 4). We can therefore be assured that there will be no endless succession of negative feelings waiting for us. For example, in the case of a divorce, there may be first a layer of despair (sadness group), then anger (at ourselves or our partner), and finally anxiety about loneliness and financial difficulties. All these emotions can be dissolved, or at least substantially reduced, with higher-consciousness healing. Anne's story illustrates how to do this.

Anne

Anne worked with higher-consciousness healing to recover from the devastating results of her recent separation from her husband. When she came to see me, she was in emotional turmoil. Her husband had left her to be with another woman, and it had come as a complete shock to her. She felt anger, grief, longing, sadness, and loneliness, and she was suffering from insomnia. In our first session, I asked her which of all these feelings was giving her the most suffering. Unfortunately, Anne was so upset that she found this question hard to answer. After talking for a while to clarify her feelings, she asked for a healing symbol to overcome her suffering from feeling despair about her divorce. She received a golden broach as her symbol. On her life-path, she saw herself halfway up the mountain, crouching, with her head down, and holding herself around the knees.

Anne cried a lot during her first two weeks of higher-consciousness healing, but she felt a genuine process of letting go. She still experienced waves of despair, but when she remembered her healing symbol, she got over these difficult emotions more quickly than before. After two weeks, she felt a bit better, but was still quite far from being happy. When she looked at her life-path, she was still crouching down, but she had stopped holding her knees and was now looking up at her higher consciousness. It wasn't a great improvement, but this imagery served as a big encouragement to her.

I asked Anne what was causing her the greatest suffering out of all her remaining symptoms. She said that although she felt less sad and despairing, she felt terrified at the prospect of living on her own. This time, she asked for a healing symbol to overcome her suffering from feeling frightened of living on her own. She worked painstakingly with her new symbol for another two weeks and her fear diminished considerably. She also started to meet up with a relative and this was a great comfort to her. When she looked at her life-path two weeks later, she was standing up and had made some tentative steps up the mountain. This improved imagery served once again as an encouragement.

I asked Anne again which of her remaining symptoms was causing her the biggest suffering. After thinking for a while, she said that the emotional hurt of being alone (sadness group) was now the worst for her. After another two weeks, she felt a lot more confident, and on her life-path, she saw that she had made even

more steps up the mountain. Once again, she selected the emotion that was causing her the biggest suffering and she asked for a symbol to overcome her suffering
from being incredibly angry about the behavior of her husband.

At the end of these eight weeks of higher-consciousness healing, Anne felt
much better. Her suffering from her divorce had dropped from 8 on the scale to
2. Her emotional state still fluctuated sometimes, but, all in all, she was over the
worst.

Each New Problem Needs a Different Symbol

We should always work with the negative emotion that is causing us the
greatest suffering in a very obvious way, just as Anne did. Each new problem and each new negative emotion needs a different healing symbol
from our higher consciousness, and we should work with each symbol for
a minimum of two weeks. After the first two weeks, we can continue with
the same symbol for as long as we feel it is helpful. Alternatively, we can
ask for another symbol for another painful emotion.

Coping with Relapses

With higher-consciousness healing, our problem will either get better
gradually over time, or suddenly and all at once. Only one thing is certain—our problem will return every now and then. Until our new healthy
pattern is deeply established, our old negative habit is bound to come
back. This is particularly true if we have had a chronic problem. In other
words, our problems rarely get better in a straight line but mostly in a zig-
zag line that gradually bends upward.

The good news is that the periods when our problem returns will get
shorter and the intervals between these periods will get longer. If we know
to expect a certain up-and-down pattern, we will feel less frustrated when
our problem comes back. Whenever a symptom comes back, just remember your healing symbol and work with it until your relapse is over. You
can do that in parallel with any other symbol that you may be working
with at the moment.

How Long Will It Take?

I used to tell my clients that they should expect to work one month for every year their problem had persisted. For example, if someone had a problem that lasted six years, they should expect to practice higher-consciousness healing for six months. However, as time went by, I realized that in most cases people achieved improvements much faster.

With regular practice, most people find that their problem either completely disappears or that it decreases to 1 or 2 on the scale of suffering after a few days, several weeks or in some cases several months. Being at 1 or 2 represents only a very small worry—and this can be seen as a reminder that nothing is perfect in the human world.

Summary

- If you have a complex problem, always start by asking for a healing symbol for the negative emotion that is bothering you the most.

- After you have finished your first two-week period of higher-consciousness healing, you can continue with the same symbol as long as you feel it is helpful.

- Alternatively, you can ask for a new healing symbol for a different problem and work with it for another two-week period.

- Each new problem and each negative emotion needs a new healing symbol.

- Relapses are a normal part of the healing process but they will get less and less with time. In case of a relapse, just go back to your initial symbol and work with it until the relapse is over.

- Most people find that their problem either completely disappears or that it decreases to 1 or 2 on the scale of suffering after a few days, several weeks, or in some cases, several months.

Chapter 14

MAKING DECISIONS WITH
LIFE-PATH IMAGERY

WE CAN USE THE IMAGERY of the life-path to help us make decisions. David's story demonstrates how that happens.

David

David wanted to change his career and was contemplating three different options. The first was to start his own business; the second was to return to his old teaching job; the third was to train as a counselor. After discussing the pros and cons of these options with him, I asked David whether he would like to consult his higher consciousness about it.

David agreed, and after he had relaxed, he asked his higher consciousness to show him his life-path and the place where he was at the moment. He saw himself a third of the way up the mountain on a narrow and steep track, ascending steadily. Then he asked what he would do on his life-path if he started his own business. Immediately, he saw himself moving hectically up and down the path. David felt that this hectic up-and-down movement symbolized the stress he would be under if he started a business, and showed him that he wouldn't make any real progress in moving closer to his higher consciousness.

Then David asked his higher consciousness what he would do on his life-path if he went back to his old teaching job. Immediately, he got a picture of himself sliding down the mountainside. This answer was clear, as well. If he went back to his old job, he would be moving backward rather than forward. All this made perfect sense to him. His third career option was counseling. When he asked his higher consciousness about this, he saw himself walking up his life-path, but it seemed a rather strenuous climb. This option seemed to be more in harmony with his path, but he felt that he wanted a job that was less strenuous.

I encouraged David not to trust these images blindly, but to check if they made sense from a commonsense point of view. David explained that they made a great deal of sense to him and that they had shown him that none of his three career options was ideal at the moment. He made the decision not to change his career until he found the type of work that would satisfy him more. Then he left the session with a good feeling.

. . .

We can test whether any area of our life is in harmony with our higher consciousness by consulting our life-path. Here is a list of questions we can ask:

What am I doing on my life-path when I do a certain job?

What am I doing on my life-path when I am in a certain relationship?

What am I doing on my life-path when I pursue a certain hobby?

What am I doing on my life-path when I follow a particular spiritual direction or teacher?

What am I doing on my life-path when I am in a certain kind of therapy?

What am I doing on my life-path when I relate to others in a certain way?

What am I doing on my life-path when I pursue a certain wish?

What am I doing on my life-path when I move to a certain town/area/house?

What am I doing on my life-path when I spend my days in a certain way?

Of course, this list is not exhaustive and you can add whatever questions are relevant to your own life. It is important to understand, however, that we must not take the answers we get to these questions as unshakable truths. Higher-consciousness healing offers us the possibility to improve our intuitive inner wisdom, but we need to be aware that in the beginning, there is the possibility of error. Therefore, always use all your intelligence and common sense to check if your inner images make sense. If you make it a habit to use the life-path imagery frequently, you are likely to develop a new and wonderful certainty about what is good for you.

Sometimes, people are a bit shocked to discover that what they are doing doesn't seem to be in harmony with their life-paths. If we discover that we have made a mistake, we should not feel depressed. On the contrary, we should celebrate our discovery. Only by recognizing our errors will we be able to take steps that will enable us to develop toward more happiness and fulfillment. Take Karen's case, for instance.

Karen

Karen decided to check whether any of her relationships were out of alignment with her higher consciousness by checking her life-path imagery. It shocked her a bit to discover that one of her closest friendships was actually causing her to go backward on her life-path.

Karen thought about this picture carefully and finally admitted to herself that she had felt more and more uncomfortable with this friendship for the past two years. She realized that she had tried to ignore these negative feelings, because she was quite attached to her friend. Now she was confronted, through her life-path imagery, with a truth she had successfully blocked out. However, once she was over her initial shock, she knew that the answer from her higher consciousness was right. Therefore, she decided to ask for a healing symbol to overcome her suffering from feeling irritation in the relationship with her friend. Through this practice, she gained more inner distance and felt much better. She still loves her friend, but she doesn't feel as unhealthily attached to her as before.

Summary

- You can use the life-path imagery to receive intuitive guidance to make decisions and to check if any area of your life is out of alignment with your higher consciousness.

- Don't trust any intuitive messages blindly. Use all your intelligence and common sense to check if they make sense.

Chapter 15

MAINTAINING WELL-BEING IN OUR LIFE

THERE IS A LOT MORE we can do with higher-consciousness healing to help us live a happy and contented life. In addition to our major personal problems, we all experience little irritations—occasional tiredness, stress, or performance anxiety. We all suffer from time to time from these issues, because they are an unavoidable by-product of being human. Luckily, with higher-consciousness healing, we can do something about most of these small problems without any great effort. The following case study shows how Robert used higher-consciousness healing for a very small problem.

Robert

Robert was offered a lift to a party. He was pleased with this, because it meant that he could have a drink. On the other hand, he knew that sitting in the back-seat of a car always made him feel sick. Robert is an enthusiastic user of higher-consciousness healing, so he at once asked for a healing symbol to overcome his suffering from feeling sick in the backseat of cars. He didn't even relax when he did this; he just asked for it shortly before he went out. He said it made a big difference and was very happy with one more success in his "self-therapy."

Standard Symbols

The following list shows issues that many people experience from time to time in a mild way. If any of these problems bothers you in a small way, you can ask for a healing symbol for it and only use it at the times when you experience this negative state of mind. These symbols are called standard symbols and you don't need to work with them for two weeks.

- Tiredness

- Stress

- Physical pain

- Nervousness or mild anxiety

- Small irritations and fears in relationships

- Feeling uninspired and dull

My own standard symbols are a golden hand for pain and a sparkling candle for tiredness. It is really nice to have these little helps at hand when I need them. It makes the unavoidable ups and downs of life seem more like smooth sailing.

Improving Our Relationships

Higher-consciousness healing is a wonderful tool to improve all our relationships and particularly those with close family members. For example, by sending love to our partner on a daily basis, it is possible to transform a "good enough marriage" into an excellent one. It is likely that we will have to sit down with our partner to discuss all our conflicts, but these conversations will be much more successful if we are armed with the tools described in this book. In the same way, we can improve the relationships with our children and loved ones.

Higher-consciousness healing can also be used to ease tensions in our everyday encounters with other people. While going about their daily activities, most people experience some awkward situations with others— tensions arising in everyday conversations or other small disruptions in their interactions with the people around them. In all these cases, we can simply visualize (or think of) the inner image of two bubbles of loving joyful light that surround us and the other person. These two bubbles may touch, but should never overlap or merge. While you are talking to the other person, travel along the boundaries of these two bubbles in your mind; this will make you feel much more secure and in control. In many cases, the effects of this short visualization are immediate and tangible. The tricky moment of the conversation is likely to pass without causing an argument; the embarrassment may subside or the feeling of being dominated may disappear. We can work in exactly the same way if we feel tormented by compulsive thoughts of difficult interactions with others. In these cases, it is often beneficial to visualize the bubble of the other person as a tiny speck on the horizon.

If your problem with the other person persists despite this short visualization, ask for a healing symbol and practice in a more concentrated way for a two-week period.

Clearing and Harmonizing Our Chakras

According to Tibetan Buddhism, we have 72,000 energy channels in our bodies, as well as five main energy centers called chakras. These chakras are located in the lower abdomen, the solar plexus, the heart, the throat, and the brain. With every thought we think, with every feeling we feel, and with every physical movement we make, energy moves through our energy channels and our chakras. If we have an emotional or physical problem, we have a disharmony in one of our chakras as well.

One way to maintain our overall well-being is to create harmony in our energy system, because it will, in turn, harmonize our mind, body, and emotions. Many people who want to work with their energy system use practices like T'ai Chi, chakra meditation, or yoga. Higher-consciousness healing offers another way of clearing, balancing, and harmonizing our main energy centers, the chakras.

If we feel a specific problem around one of our chakras—a lump in our throat or a tension in our chest—we can ask for a healing symbol to overcome our suffering from this blockage in the usual way. But here comes something new: healing symbols to harmonize the chakras are not all visualized in the heart, but in the specific chakra with which we are working. If, for example, we want to work on a block in our throat chakra, we visualize our healing symbol in our throat. We let the light of our healing symbol expand from our throat and fill our body and a bubble of loving light around ourselves. If we are working on our navel chakra, we visualize our healing symbol in our navel and let the light expand from there. We should work with these healing symbols in the usual way for two minutes, twice a day, for two weeks.

Katie

Katie is an experienced meditator and had practiced chakra meditations for some time. She felt that most of her chakras were "clear," but she often suffered from an uncomfortable lump in her throat, accompanied by feelings of anxiety. Her healing symbol was shown to her as a bright golden sun. She visualized this golden sun in her throat and expanded its light all through her body and beyond. After practicing for a few days, she felt the lump in her throat melting and the feelings of anxiety decreasing. She recognized that she always felt this lump when she feared that she couldn't connect with other people in the way she wanted. Katie found these insights interesting and carried on practicing her healing symbol. She found that often the mere thought of her healing symbol was enough to stop the lump in her throat from returning. Simultaneously, her ability to relate to others improved.

Experimenting with Higher-Consciousness Healing

I want to encourage everyone to experiment with higher-consciousness healing on any problem or challenge that has not been covered in this book. There will never be a danger of making an issue worse, because the heart of higher-consciousness healing is love. Here is another case story that illustrates the effects of higher-consciousness healing on one of the learning disorders in children that have become epidemic over recent years.

Martha

Martha asked me if she could use higher-consciousness healing for her nine-year-old son Robert, who had been diagnosed with dyspraxia at the age of seven. At that age Robert could not ride a bike, catch a ball, or swim—despite years of swimming lessons. His parents had then gone through a lengthy course of physiotherapy with Robert that had improved his condition somewhat. But at age nine, Robert was still far away from being good at sports, and his handwriting was still two years behind what was expected of him. I told Martha that I was no expert in learning disorders, but I encouraged her to experiment with higher-consciousness healing as it could do no harm. At a minimum, I said, it could help Robert to alleviate the social and emotional problems resulting from his condition. Martha and her husband practiced higher-consciousness healing for their son by visualizing a bright sun in his brain for six months—two minutes daily. To their great surprise, Robert's handwriting improved so much that he is now a year ahead of his class. He also became very good at his chosen sports. Robert's parents, as well as his schoolteacher, were stunned by this unlikely development.

Summary

- You can work with symbols on very small issues like occasional pain, stress, or tiredness with standard symbols. Just use these symbols when your problem becomes acute.

- You can use higher-consciousness healing to improve all your important relationships by sending these people love on a regular basis.

- You can alleviate occasional tensions in contact with others by visualizing a bubble of love around each of you.

- Higher-consciousness healing can be used to clear away blocks and disharmonies in your chakras. Ask in the usual way for a healing symbol, but visualize your symbol in the chakra with which you are working. Let its light and color expand from there.

- You are encouraged to experiment with higher-consciousness healing on any problem that has not been covered. Higher-consciousness healing can never make any problem worse.

Chapter 16

THE ULTIMATE HEALING SYMBOL

YOU MAY ALREADY HAVE GUESSED IT. The ultimate healing symbol is your higher consciousness itself. You can use this symbol in exactly the same way you use your other healing symbols. Visualize (or sense) your higher consciousness in a pleasing form and in very beautiful radiant colors in your heart and breathe its good qualities and color first to yourself. Envelop yourself with a bubble of love. Then breathe the loving light from your higher consciousness to others (your loved ones, as well as those you find particularly difficult at the moment) and envelop them with bubbles of love as well. If you start and end your days with this simple visualization, you will find that your life becomes happier and more successful in every respect, and that obstacles disappear more readily.

Working with the symbol of our higher consciousness will help us with a kind of suffering that no kind of psychotherapy can alleviate—the suffering that stems from the fact that we are separated from our higher consciousness. Even if we live in the best of all circumstances—with a fantastic career, the best of all partners, as much money as we want, and whatever else is important to us—in the back of our mind, we know that we will lose all this one day. Our family might die today in a car accident; tomorrow, we might be sacked from our job. No matter how hard we try to ignore this insight, there is no real security to be found in this world.

Another problem that we share with almost every human being is that nothing can completely satisfy us for long. Even if our deepest wishes are fulfilled, it is unlikely that the thrill of this fulfillment will last more than a few months. After that time, we become used to our new situation and our deep-seated dissatisfaction will resurface and ask for "more" and "better."

Most of us are not fully aware of these kinds of problems, because we are so used to them. But if we don't realize that we are suffering from this "spiritual illness," we tend to project our inner restlessness and deep-seated anxiety onto our partner, onto our job, or onto our other life circumstances. We just don't realize that no human condition can give us what we long for most deeply and most intensely—the recognition that we already possess the infinite love, happiness, and wisdom of our higher consciousness. Working with the symbol of our higher consciousness will bring us nearer to realizing this truth.

Amanda

Amanda had successfully used higher-consciousness healing to dissolve her chronic tiredness and her anxieties around money. However, she still experienced what she called a "mental fog" that led to confusion and social clumsiness. This was a very stubborn problem that she had had virtually all her adult life. Amanda had browsed through many different images of deities on the Internet. At some point, she found an image of the Chinese goddess of compassion Kwan Yin, who inspired her greatly. She immediately decided to visualize her higher consciousness in the form of Kwan Yin. (Before, she had simply visualized a brilliant light.) The image of Kwan Yin had a powerful effect on Amanda's mind. It brought an amount of mental sharpness that was new to her and the incidences of "mental fog" decreased. Simultaneously, Amanda felt that she found more of her "true self"—a deep inner sense of love and security that was not conditioned by anything outside herself.

Summary

- The ultimate healing symbol is the symbol of your higher consciousness itself. Always visualize your higher consciousness in a beautiful and radiantly colorful form.

- You can work with the symbol of your higher consciousness in exactly the same way as you work with your other healing symbols.

- Working with the symbol of your higher consciousness will help you realize the unconditional happiness of your true nature.

Chapter 17

MANIFESTING OUR DREAMS

MOST PEOPLE FIND THAT their problems and negative emotions readily decrease once they work with the loving light of their healing symbols. Once we have reached 1 or 2 on the scale of suffering, it is time to start working on manifesting our dreams. Ways to do this are described in a huge number of self-help books that have become very popular in recent years. Unfortunately, despite this popularity, many people still struggle to put these teachings into practice. Having used these techniques with great success myself over the past twenty years, I will try to clarify their most important points.

The core of manifesting our dreams is to trust that our wishes will manifest. In order to do this, we must suspend our ordinary ideas about time and space. However, it is not enough simply to visualize our dreams or to think positively, even though this will be helpful. In order to build genuine trust, we must experience *sustained enthusiastic desire* for what we want. This burning desire—if maintained over months and even years—will result in unshakable trust and this trust works like a magnet that attracts into our life whatever we want.

It is obvious that in order to sustain enthusiastic desire over a long period of time we need to have a happy and enthusiastic mind. Therefore, strong negative feelings work like big blockages to fulfilling our dreams. For example, we can try to visualize a soul-mate or a successful career for a very long time, but if we are full of bitterness and despair, we are unlikely to get anywhere with this technique. Therefore, when we are engulfed in negative emotions, it is paramount to reduce those feelings first with a healing symbol before we can expect to get good results by visualizing our aims.

Altruistic Love

In principle, achieving our aims is extremely simple. It can be summarized in one single sentence: Clearly define your aim and enthusiastically focus on it in an ongoing way. Unfortunately, despite this simplicity, most people experience a host of obstacles when they are confronted with an unfulfilled desire. They may feel undeserving; they may feel hopeless; they may feel under-confident. They may also think that their wish is unrealistic; they may not believe in the power of their minds; they may even believe that focusing on their wishes is selfish and sinful. Above all, they may feel impatience, which is a subtle form of anger.

> **Clearly define your aim and enthusiastically focus on it.**

I will now share with you my personal secret for overcoming all these obstacles that has worked wonderfully in my own life. The most important key to successful manifestation is to combine our personal desires with altruistic love for all beings. For example, instead of simply wishing to have a successful business, we should concentrate on the wish to benefit all beings with our products. In that way, our own success will be a welcome "by-product." Instead of simply wishing for a partner, we should wish for being part of such a loving couple that our happiness will make many other people happy as well. Obviously, in that way, we will also find a gorgeous partner.

Altruistic love will help us fulfill our wishes more quickly, because wishing for everyone will dissolve our feelings of unworthiness, impatience, and doubt. Instead, we will feel more confident, deserving, and enthusiastic. It is exactly this enthusiastic state of mind that will make it most likely that our wishes will be fulfilled. Moreover, wishing with love will protect us from going on a selfish ego trip and desiring things that can't bring happiness. For example, most people realize that simply being rich and famous doesn't bring any happiness per se. Just open any celebrity magazine to see that many rich and famous people have terrible problems. But living in a state of altruistic love will make us very happy, no matter what we do for a living. If you are in doubt whether your wishes will bring you happiness, you can always consult the life-path imagery as explained in chapter 14.

Freeing Ourselves from Grudges and Guilt

In my life-coaching practice I have observed that feelings like resentment and guilt work as almost insurmountable barriers to fulfilling our dreams. It's almost as if someone says, "You can either have your old grudges and guilt feelings or you can fulfill your dreams. You can't have both." This is particularly true if we block out these negative feelings.

Therefore, in order to undo any conscious or unconscious obstacles of guilt or resentment, we should first send love to everyone who was and still is important to us—including our parents, ex-partners, our children (including all babies that have not been carried to term), and to all our present important relationships. We should visualize these people one by one in front of our inner eye and wish them to be happy and healthy in every respect. If our love flows freely and joyfully we can rejoice because we are free of inner barriers to fulfilling our dreams.

However, if negative feelings like anger, grief, or guilt arise, we should use higher-consciousness healing until we can wholeheartedly send the other person our loving wishes. If at all possible we should let the other person know that we have let go of our grudges toward them and we should also make amends wherever possible when we have treated someone else badly.

After doing this sometimes difficult but all-important work, we are free to embark on the life of our dreams.

How to Visualize

It is important to visualize your aim as much as possible. The simple formula is: What you can imagine you can have; what you can't imagine you can't have. However, it is important that we do not try to force our inner images. Instead, we should look out for all of our inner doubts and insecurities that may come up if we imagine the life of our dreams. If we notice even the most shadowy resistance we should change and improve our inner imagery in order to "take care" of these inner barriers. For example, one client of mine wished for a boyfriend. Unfortunately, she wasn't very enthusiastic about this wish because she had deep fears that no man would stay with her. So I suggested that she imagine that her boyfriend proposed to her. First, my client was almost shocked at this suggestion, but once she started to imagine it, she found that it would indeed alleviate her fears. She then became very excited and enthusiastic about her dream to have a loving relationship—which is just the right attitude that makes it much more likely that she will succeed.

The Technique for Manifesting Your Dreams: Defining Your Wish

- Clearly write down, in as much detail as possible, what you want to achieve. If other people are involved in your aim, remember that they have free will. Simply wish for them to be happy and do not impose your wishes on them.

- Make sure that you have as much to give as you want to receive. For example, if you wish for a very loving partner, make sure that you are very loving yourself. If you want to earn a large amount of money by selling a certain product, make sure that your product is worth this amount of money.

- Think of as many ways as possible that you can benefit others with the fulfillment of your wish. Write all this down.

Visualizing Your Wish

- Close your eyes, relax, and generate a positive and happy feeling in yourself. Focus on this positive feeling until you feel truly joyful.

- Perceive yourself as beautiful and radiantly healthy. Really enjoy your body (do not think that you are merely imagining it.)

- Radiate love to everyone around you. Really experience the loving feeling.

- See yourself in your ideal situation, which contains, in symbolic form, all aspects of your wish. (For example, see yourself in a beautiful home, surrounded by loving relationships, with tokens of your achievement apparent—an image of a successful work project, etc.) Deeply enjoy this experience and feel that what you visualize is really true at this present moment.

- See yourself surrounded by all the people you want to benefit with your wish (for example, happy family members, customers, patients, clients, children, friends, students, etc.)

- See your higher consciousness above the entire scene, blessing it with a loving smile. Deeply enjoy this experience and see it as complete reality.

- Look out for any (shadowy) doubts or anxieties about achieving your aim. If you detect any insecurities, change and improve your visualization until it becomes ideal. (This step is very important. The more inner obstacles you can find and eliminate the better.)

- All this manifests now for the best of all beings.

We should work with these images every day for at least five to ten minutes. In fact, the more we think about our aim the better. If we can focus on our aim with ongoing enthusiasm, we will feel as happy as if we had already received our wish. It is very important to talk about our dream only to people who are fully supportive.

We may be lucky and receive the fulfillment of our wish in a matter of weeks, but in most cases, we will have to be more patient to see results. It is precisely this waiting time that can bring up many negative feelings—hopelessness, impatience, and even despair. If this happens, work once again with higher-consciousness healing to dissolve these painful emotions. As I said before, the manifestation technique will only bring results if we can maintain our enthusiasm as long as it takes to manifest our dream. Therefore, the happier we are, the more likely our wish will be fulfilled.

It is also very important to stay with the same aim throughout. Think of the process as sowing seeds. If we sow one seed one day, only to dig it up repeatedly and replace it with another, we will never manage to harvest the fruits of our efforts.

Finally, we must do everything that common sense dictates to achieve our aim. For example, if we wish for a partner, it doesn't make sense to stay at home and watch television every day. Equally, if we want to become a successful artist, it will not happen by visualization alone. We also have to practice, attend schools, and try to exhibit our works.

My Own Experiences

I am a big fan of manifestation techniques and have been using them with great success for over twenty years. When I started, my results were slow and not very impressive, because I did not truly believe in the power of my mind. Also, I didn't know any better and gave in to my negative feelings when they arose. Above all, I was full of self-pity about my childhood experienes of neglect and abuse. All this changed when I experienced a shocking betrayal by my boyfriend that jolted me out of my self-pitying complacency. The extreme pain of this experience slowly transformed into a steely determination to have only "good" relationships. Four years later (it felt like an eternity at the time), I met my future husband and he became my deeply beloved soul-mate. From then on, I didn't allow any aspect of my life to develop by chance. Career, family, home, emotions, health, and spiritual development—I have had very precise aims for all these areas and I still do. Over the years, I have been able to "tick off" wish after wish, while benefiting more and more people in the process. For example, higher-consciousness healing is the result of my wish to find an extraordinarily effective therapeutic technique that has the potential to benefit everyone. The ongoing good feedback from my clients and readers continues to make me deeply happy and grateful. This does not mean, however, that my life now is completely free from challenges—far from it. It just means that with my daily practice of higher-consciousness healing and manifestation techniques I get over most of these problems more easily.

Summary

- Once you have reduced your suffering to 1 or 2 on the scale with higher-consciousness healing, you can start manifesting your positive aims.

- Always combine your personal aims with the wish to benefit all beings in the process.

- Eliminate old grudges and guilt feelings by sending love to everyone who was and is important to you.

- Define your wish as clearly as possible and visualize a key image that contains all aspects of it.

- Watch out for any (shadowy) doubts and insecurities and eliminate these obstacles by improving your inner image until it becomes ideal.

- Focus on your aim with sustained enthusiasm.

- Only talk about your dream to people who are fully supportive.

- If strong negative emotions arise, use higher-consciousness healing to dissolve them.

- Do everything that common sense dictates to achieve your aim.

Chapter 18

HEALING OTHERS

HIGHER-CONSCIOUSNESS HEALING offers a unique and highly effective technique we can use to help our loved ones and the world in general. Before I explain in detail how to do this, let me first share the results Barbara achieved by using the method to help herself, her husband, and her daughter.

Barbara

Barbara contacted me because she was on the brink of divorce from her husband. They argued every day and their sex life was nonexistent. I showed Barbara how to send love to herself and to her husband with the help of a healing symbol. When she came back, she reported that she had stopped arguing with her husband and that she was able to value him more. She had also been able to be more assertive about some long-standing issues and had achieved a good compromise. After another two weeks, Barbara told me that she and her husband had fallen in love again and had rekindled their sex life. Obviously, her husband was over the moon, even though he didn't know anything about higher-consciousness healing.

Then Barbara told me about the terrible tantrums of her four-year-old son that drove her mad. She received a healing symbol (a light blue child's bed) and practiced it for another two weeks on behalf of her son. She visualized him in front of her inner eye and saw the blue child's bed in his heart. Then she imagined the blue light radiating into his little body and all around him, filling him with love. To her joy, her son improved dramatically and only rarely had a tantrum from then on. All these improvements were stable and lasting.

...

We should only practice higher-consciousness healing on behalf of someone else if we feel loving and positive toward this person. By contrast, if we feel negative emotions toward a person, we must work on our own painful feelings first. For example, if we are annoyed that our partner is miserable and depressed, we should first work with a healing symbol on our own annoyance. Often, this will simultaneously have a healing effect on our partner. It is important to understand that this change does not come about through some sort of secret manipulation, but through the working of our higher consciousness, which always acts in the best interest of everyone concerned. Once we feel loving and positive toward the other person, we can help them by practicing higher-consciousness healing on their behalf, as Sheila did with her son.

Sheila

For years Sheila had not properly communicated with her adult son who had a drug problem. She worried a lot about him and had successfully reduced this negative feeling with a healing symbol. When she talked to me, she felt more confident and peaceful, but her son was just as withdrawn and miserable as before. So she decided to use a healing symbol on his behalf and practiced it with all her heart. To her extreme surprise, her son came to her house a few days later and voluntarily started to talk about his problems—something he had never done before. Sheila was overjoyed, and from then on, their relationship improved a great deal.

...

There are three different ways to use higher-consciousness healing to help others: by joining in their practice, and by practicing on their behalf, either with or without their knowledge.

Joining Others in Their Practice

We can help those who are already working with healing symbols by joining them in their practice. First, we should ask them which healing symbol they have received from their higher consciousness and listen carefully to the description. Then we visualize the other person in front of us and see or sense their healing symbol in *their* hearts. When we breathe out, we visualize the color of their symbols radiating out from their hearts and filling their bodies and their whole surroundings with love. Love means to wish them to be happy and healthy with all our heart. It does not mean, however, to have specific ideas about what they should do (e.g., "I wish my son goes to law school and gets married"), because that would be violating their right to choose for themselves.

We practice in this way for two minutes, twice a day, for two weeks, exactly as we would with our own symbol. In my experience, when two friends or a couple work together in this way, the results of higher-consciousness healing can be even more dramatic.

Helping Others with Their Knowledge

Generally speaking, it's better to teach others the simple practice of higher-consciousness healing than it is to practice it on their behalf, because helping people to help themselves is the most empowering kind of support. However, in some cases, people may feel too weak or ill. In the case of children, they may be too young to work with the method. In these cases, the other person may be very grateful if we offer to practice higher-consciousness healing on his or her behalf. In order to do this, we must first clarify what emotion the other person wants to overcome, as described in chapter 4. Then we ask our own higher consciousness for a healing symbol on behalf of the other person. Once we are relaxed, ask in the following way:

Please give me a healing symbol for (name) that will help her/him to overcome her/his suffering from (feeling) about (problem).

Then we practice the healing symbol on behalf of the other person as described in previous section.

Once children are of school age, we can start to teach them how to use higher-consciousness healing themselves. At first, we may still have to ask for a symbol on their behalf, but we can make a simple drawing of the symbol and ask them to join us in the visualization. As they grow older, they will be able to do more and more higher-consciousness healing by themselves.

Emma

Ten-year-old Emma felt excluded and picked on at school. Her teacher was very supportive, but the situation did not improve for several months. Therefore, Emma's mother helped her to receive a symbol and sat next to Emma as she practiced it each night before bed. Then Emma did something she had never done before. For two days she did not try to play with her difficult classmates but joined some younger children in their play. On the third day she returned to her old playmates. To her delight, she noticed that suddenly all the difficulties had stopped. This development was stable and lasting.

Helping Others without Their Knowledge

In some cases, it is impossible to ask people for consent to use higher-consciousness healing on their behalf. We may care deeply for a family member, but never have talked to them about their personal problems. Or we may fear that the other person will reject higher-consciousness healing. In either case, we can still practice the method on their behalf and be sure that our practice will only work in the highest interest of the other person. As long as we ask our higher consciousness for a healing symbol exactly in the way outlined in the previous section and use it with love, there is no danger of imposing our personal will on other people. As I have explained before, we all share higher consciousness, even though it may appear to us in many different forms and shapes.

Practicing higher-consciousness healing on behalf of small children is extremely rewarding. To my joy, I have known toddlers who slept through the night for the first time in years, and children who stopped having tantrums and became happy and co-operative instead.

When we work with higher-consciousness healing on behalf of others, we ask for a healing symbol and practice it as outlined in the previous two sections. If we do not know from which negative emotion our friend or relative suffers, we simply ask for a healing symbol to help the other person to overcome his or her unhappiness.

Jake

The mother of four-year-old Jake contacted me because her son was very afraid of going to school. He was attending nursery school, but he always became very emotional when his parents tried to talk to him about going to elementary school. His parents promised him a lovely present for his first day at school, but it didn't help. I helped Jake's mother receive a healing symbol on his behalf to overcome his anxiety. She received a bright-red toy fireman as a symbol. After practicing with it for a week, she and Jake drove past his intended elementary school and said, as usual, what a lovely school it was. To her immense surprise, Jake announced confidently that this was his favorite school and he was looking forward to going there in the summer. From that moment, Jake's fear of going to school disappeared.

Summary

- You must feel positive and loving toward someone if you want to help with higher-consciousness healing. If you are involved in the problem, you must dissolve your own negative emotions first.

- You can join others in their practice of higher-consciousness healing in order to increase their results.

- If you practice higher-consciousness healing on behalf of others, ask for a symbol in the following way: *Please give me a healing symbol for (name) that will help her/him to overcome her/his suffering from (feeling) about (problem).*

- Visualize those you want to help in front of you and see their symbol in their hearts, radiating healing light into their bodies and enveloping them in a bubble of love.

- Only wish for others to be happy and healthy. Do not specify how the other person should live as this would violate their right to choose for themselves.

Chapter 19

PASSING ON THE POWER

WOULD YOU LIKE TO PASS HIGHER-CONSCIOUSNESS healing on to your friends? Would you like to use it in your counseling or healing practice or teach it in evening classes and workshops? You can. You have my explicit permission to do so. However, in order to be a confident teacher of the method, you must first achieve a few real personal successes solving your own problems. "Real" success means that you have practiced higher-consciousness healing on at least two personal issues in exactly the way I describe in this book, and that you now score no more than 1 or 2 on the scale of suffering. Your life-path imagery should also have improved accordingly. With your own success in the back of your mind, you will be an empathetic therapist who radiates genuine optimism and a teacher who can inspire students.

It is my deep wish that as many people as possible benefit from higher-consciousness healing. If you feel inspired by this method, I warmly invite you to support this aim. In my vision, I see people all over the globe solving their debilitating and crippling problems. I see children in school being taught this simple method and I see everyone much happier and more confident. Tiny sparks of light grow stronger; they grow together and spread. When we are happier and more loving as individuals, we influence our whole environment in a positive way. We bring peace and happiness into our families, to our workplaces, to our communities, and, finally, to the whole world. It is a grand aim, but we have to start with ourselves.

When you pass higher-consciousness healing on to others, please don't change the method in any way. Even the smallest details are important.

Also, if you use higher-consciousness healing with your clients, always make them aware that this is a self-help method they can use on their own as soon as they are ready and give credit to this book. Sadly, I once met a therapist who had learned the method from this book, but only gave his clients symbols he had asked for on their behalf. This may have increased his earnings by making his clients more dependent on him, but it is not truly empowering. I also found a website on the Internet advertising higher-consciousness healing and offering symbols for people to use without giving credit to this book. This is not how I want people to spread this method. Please make sure that you pass on higher-consciousness healing in the self-help spirit in which it is offered.

Study groups and self-help groups are also great ways to practice higher-consciousness healing with others. Self-help groups are very empowering, because they give everyone the additional boost of confidence that comes from being able to help themselves.

You can start a self-help group by meeting with just one friend. I am sure that after only a short time, your work will attract more friends who want to find out why you are suddenly able to solve the problems in your life one after another. Here are some suggestions for running a self-help group:

Rotate the leadership of the group each time you meet.

- Use this book or a tape to guide you through the practice in order to receive new symbols.

- Share your experiences with higher-consciousness healing and listen to each other, but do not give each other advice unless someone explicitly asks for it.

You can visit my website at *www.taraspringett.com*, where you can join the higher-consciousness healing community and share your experiences. May all your problems be resolved. I wish you the best of luck.

THE COMPLETE PRACTICE OF
HIGHER-CONSCIOUSNESS HEALING

Preparation

- Identify the negative emotion around your problem (anger, sadness or anxiety) and define your problem in this form: *My suffering from (emotion) about (problem).* Write this definition down.

- Measure, on a scale from 0 to 10, how much, on average, you suffer from the negative emotion (anger, sadness, anxiety) about your problem. (0 is no suffering at all; 5 is a good deal of suffering; 7 indicates the beginnings of despair; 10 is utter desperation). Write this number down.

- Do the following practice in relaxation. Most people find it easy to read paragraph for paragraph and imagine what has been said. Alternatively, ask someone to read you through the relaxation exercise below. You could even make your own tape.

Relaxation

- Sit or lie down comfortably, and undo all tight clothing. You can put your hands on your stomach to feel the movement of your breathing. Every time you breathe in, feel your hands rise slightly; every time you breathe out, feel your hands fall slightly. Let yourself fall into the out breath and relax your whole being.

- You are now going on a journey through your whole body. Start with your feet. Bring your awareness into your feet and feel inside your feet. Let all tensions fall away with your out breath. Now feel into your lower legs and let all tensions fall away with your out breath. Do the same with your thighs, your abdomen, your stomach, your chest, your shoulders, your arms, your neck, your face, your whole head. Your whole being is now wonderfully relaxed. Enjoy that feeling.

- Now sink even more deeply into relaxation and, as you count from 1 to 10, see yourself going down a stairway toward a beautiful and secure place. As you say each number, take one step down, sinking deeper and deeper into relaxation: 1, 2, deeper and deeper; . . . 3, 4, deeper still; . . . 5, 6, 7, deeper; . . . 8, and deeper; . . . 9, 10. . . .

- You have arrived at your beautiful place and you are completely safe here. Find somewhere to make yourself comfortable.

Meeting Your Higher Consciousness

- You are now ready to contact your higher consciousness. This is the part of yourself that is completely loving and wise, and already knows the answer to all your questions. At the same time, it is outside yourself and you share it with everyone else. Your personal higher consciousness is also the higher consciousness of the whole universe. Imagine your higher consciousness as a living shimmering light, as an angelic being surrounded by brilliant light, or as a central figure of the religion you follow.

- See and feel your higher consciousness coming nearer. You can feel how its beams of love surround you and care for you. You can sense how you yourself become more loving and joyful when you are touched by its wonderful presence. It is a symbol of your highest potential. To move toward it and finally unite with it is both your ultimate task and your goal in life. Doing this will bring you the kind of joy and happiness that doesn't depend on outer conditions and can't be taken away from you.

- Now you are ready to explore your life-path. Remember that this is entirely optional. If you choose not to use the life-path imagery, go on to the next step of asking for a healing symbol.

Exploring Your Life-Path

- See your higher consciousness on top of a mountain and ask it to show you a path, a track, or a road leading toward the mountaintop.

- When you can see this path, ask your higher consciousness: *Can you please show me where I am on this path?*

- When you have received the answer, remember that it doesn't matter whether you are still down in the valley or whether you are already halfway up the mountain. All that matters is that you are moving toward your higher consciousness and that you are unfolding its wonderful qualities.

- Ask your higher consciousness to show you what you are doing on your life-path when you experience your problem. For example, you may be straying from your path, walking in place, or going downhill. Whatever is shown to you, don't judge yourself. Ask your higher consciousness: *Please, can you show me what I am doing on my life-path when I suffer from feeling (emotion) about (problem)?*

- Thank your higher consciousness for the answer.

Asking for Your Healing Symbol

- Ask your higher consciousness to show you a healing symbol to overcome your problem. It may be something like a gemstone, a flower, or a geometrical form. You may be shown one or several symbols. Pick the one that feels best for you. It must have a beautiful form and color. Ask in the following way: *Please give me a healing symbol to overcome my suffering from (emotion) about (problem).*

- If you like the symbol, thank your higher consciousness. If you do not really like the symbol, ask for another one.

Working with Your Symbol

- See or sense your healing symbol in the openness of your heart in the middle of your chest. While you breathe out, radiate the color and positive qualities of your healing symbol throughout your whole body and surround it with a bubble of loving joyful light the size of your outstretched arms. It is a loving and healing light that brings comfort, clarity, and happiness. Feel all tensions and negative emotions melt away in the loving light of your symbol. The bubble of love has a clear and firm boundary.

- Wish yourself to be happy with all your heart and say to yourself: I wish myself to be happy.

- If you find it difficult to send love to yourself, think first about someone you find easy to love and wish them to be happy. Without changing this feeling, turn it toward yourself and wish yourself to be happy with all your heart. Alternately, think of your higher consciousness sending you love.

- If other people are involved in your problem, breathe the color to them as well. See the person in front of you and feel how the loving joyful light from your healing symbol forms a bubble of love around him or her. Your bubbles of light may touch, but should not overlap. In your mind, say to this person: I wish you to be happy. Know that everyone who is genuinely happy immediately repents their wrongdoings and becomes very likeable.

- If you feel resentment toward your parents, always envelop them in bubbles of loving light as well.

- If you feel guilty toward the person who is involved in your problem, say: I am sorry for what I did. I wish you to be happy.

- If you feel regrets toward the person who is involved in your problem, say: I am sorry it didn't work out. I wish you to be happy.

- Notice if you still feel any negative emotion. If yes, notice where in your physical body you feel the tensions that go along with this negative emotion.

- Direct the healing light of your symbol to the part of your body where you feel the tensions of your negative emotion and relax these tensions with each out breath. You can imagine these tensions as a tight flower bud that opens into a beautiful bloom with each out breath.

- Sometimes, tensions are in more than one place in your body. Relax all these tensions, one after the other, until your whole body is completely relaxed and your negative emotions are completely dissolved.

- Work in the same way with fatigue or physical pain.

- If you feel any form of fear or anxiety, use the antianxiety breathing technique at the same time.

- If you feel sad or depressed, practice with a smile on your face.

- When you are ready, open your eyes.

Daily Life

- Work with your healing symbol for two minutes, twice daily, for a minimum of two weeks, and every time your negative thoughts and feelings arise. Instead of dwelling on negative self-talk and painful emotions, put your mind immediately on your healing symbol and breathe out its color to surround yourself and others with bubbles of loving joyful light. Simultaneously, put a smile on your face and relax the tensions of your negative emotions.

- Continue to work in this way no matter what happens—good or bad—and never change your symbol. At the same time, put into practice any insight you receive on how to solve and improve your problem.

- After two weeks, measure your improvements on the scale of suffering using the same precise definition of your problem, and tune into your life-path imagery to check for any improvements. Try to appreciate even the smallest decrease in suffering.

I'd love to hear about your success stories. Visit my website at

www.taraspringett.com

to let me know about your experience with the method.

About the Author

TARA SPRINGETT is a psychotherapist and the author of several self-help books (published in the UK and Europe) that combine psychological insight with Buddhist wisdom. She has been a deeply committed Tibetan Buddhist practitioner since 1985 and an authorized teacher since 1994, and has been working with meditation students and counseling clients for more than twenty years.

TO OUR READERS

Weiser Books, an imprint of Red Wheel/Weiser, publishes books across the entire spectrum of occult and esoteric subjects. Our mission is to publish quality books that will make a difference in people's lives without advocating any one particular path or field of study. We value the integrity, originality, and depth of knowledge of our authors.

Our readers are our most important resource, and we appreciate your input, suggestions, and ideas about what you would like to see published. Please feel free to contact us to request our latest book catalog, or to be added to our mailing list.

Red Wheel/Weiser, LLC
500 Third Street, Suite 230
San Francisco, CA 94107
www.redwheelweiser.com